FRESH *and* LIGHT

photography by William Meppem

FRESH *and* LIGHT
Copyright © 2013 by Donna Hay
All rights reserved
Photographs copyright © William Meppem 2012
Author and styling: Donna Hay
Art direction and design: Chi Lam
Copy editor: Melanie Hansche
Recipe testing: Hannah Meppem

Published by HarperCollins Publishers Ltd
First Canadian edition

HarperCollins books may be purchased for educational, business, or
sales promotional use through our Special Markets Department.

HarperCollins Publishers Ltd
2 Bloor Street East, 20th Floor
Toronto, Ontario, Canada
M4W 1A8

www.harpercollins.ca

Library and Archives Canada Cataloguing in Publication information is available upon request.

ISBN 978-1-44342-407-3

on the cover
lemon chicken with tomato salad, page 65

Reproduction by News PreMedia Centre
Printed in China by RR Donnelley on 157gsm Matt Art

HCANZ 9 8 7 6 5 4 3 2 1

donna hay

FRESH *and* LIGHT

180+ new recipes and flavour-packed ideas to find the perfect balance

HarperCollins*Publishers*Ltd

CONTENTS

*Ingredients marked with an asterisk have a glossary entry

INTRODUCTION

I've never been a fan of diets and I don't even like the idea of anyone being on a diet. So this is not a diet book. For me, it's always been about balance, and *Fresh and Light* is my answer to my own best efforts at juggling for that perfect balance. It's about a flavour-packed yet lighter touch, leaving room for the little indulgences in life.

Designed to complement my existing repertoire, it's full of new recipes that combine the freshest ingredients, pantry staples and a few personal tricks for a lighter approach. Divided by meal, *Fresh and Light* is loaded with power foods to give you energy over the nights of the week you really need it. With a focus on vegetables, grains and proteins, I've used ingredients such as whole-wheat flour and whole grains that you might need to track down in a health food store, but with good reason. It's all about flavour and eating well.

We all have our guilty pleasures in life. This book isn't about denying them. It lets you enjoy them and is for those times when you're seeking something a little more virtuous. And that's really the best kind of indulgence of all – the one with balance. I hope this book helps you find yours. As always, happy cooking!

E-BOOK

While I'll never lose my passion for the printed page and the tactile nature of a book, I'm equally excited by the digital version. I'm overjoyed that *Fresh and Light* will be my first book available in digital format. Complete with step-by-step cook modes, each recipe is broken into a slideshow of steps that enlarge to allow the user to easily follow a recipe while they are cooking. For an exclusive sneak peek at the e-book, visit donnahay.com

Donna

BREAKFAST

We all know how EASY it is to skip breakfast. Sometimes just grabbing a coffee on the RUN seems like enough. (I used to think it was the breakfast of champions!) So this is my antidote to all those missed breakfasts. There are FAST treats full of energy and GOODNESS you can have on the fly, as well as more SUBSTANTIAL meals packed with whole grains, protein and loads of flavour.

BREAKFAST BARS

WHOLE-WHEAT HONEY *and* RICOTTA PANCAKES

BREAKFAST BARS

¾ cup (65g) rolled oats
¼ cup (20g) flaked almonds
¼ cup (35g) sunflower seeds
¼ cup (25g) quinoa flakes*
2 tablespoons wheat germ*
⅔ cup (100g) plain (all-purpose) whole-wheat flour*
½ teaspoon baking powder
⅔ cup (120g) brown sugar
1 teaspoon ground cinnamon
½ cup (125ml) canola or vegetable oil
1 egg
1 teaspoon vanilla extract
1 cup (130g) dried cranberries

Preheat oven to 160°C (325°F). Place the oats, almonds, sunflower seeds and quinoa flakes on a baking tray lined with non-stick baking paper and bake for 10 minutes, stirring occasionally, or until light golden. Allow to cool.

Place the wheat germ, flour, baking powder, brown sugar and cinnamon in a bowl and stir to combine. Add the oil, egg and vanilla and stir until smooth. Add the oat mixture and cranberries and stir to combine. Spoon the mixture into a 20cm x 30cm slice tin lined with non-stick baking paper. Bake for 25–30 minutes or until golden brown. Cool in the tin for 10 minutes before turning on to a wire rack to cool completely. Cut into bars to serve. MAKES 16
+ These bars will keep in an airtight container for up to 1 week.

WHOLE-WHEAT HONEY
and RICOTTA PANCAKES

1 cup (150g) plain (all-purpose) whole-wheat flour*
2 teaspoons baking powder
¼ cup (90g) honey, plus extra, to serve
⅔ cup (160ml) milk
150g reduced-fat ricotta, plus extra, to serve
3 eggwhites

Place the flour and baking powder in a bowl and mix to combine. Make a well in the centre, add the honey and milk and mix until smooth. Gently fold through the ricotta so the mixture is still a little lumpy. Place the eggwhites in a clean bowl and whisk until soft peaks form. Fold the eggwhites through the ricotta mixture.

Heat a large non-stick frying pan over low heat. Spray the pan with cooking spray and add 2 tablespoonsful of the mixture into the pan. Cook, in batches, for 3–4 minutes each side or until golden and puffed. Serve with extra ricotta and honey. SERVES 4

FIVE-GRAIN PORRIDGE

1 cup (90g) rolled oats
1 cup (90g) rolled spelt oats*
1 cup (90g) rolled barley*
¾ cup (150g) white quinoa*
½ cup (85g) linseeds*
1½ cups (375ml) water
2 cups (500ml) milk
sea salt flakes
extra milk and honey, to serve

Combine the rolled oats, spelt oats, barley, quinoa and linseeds[+]. To make the porridge, place 1 cup of the mixture in a saucepan with the water and milk. Cook over medium heat, stirring frequently, for 6–8 minutes or until the grains are tender. Stir through a pinch of salt. Spoon into bowls and serve with extra milk and honey.
SERVES 2–4
+ This is the base of the five-grain porridge. It will keep in an airtight jar for up to 3 weeks.

BASIC MUFFIN

2 cups (300g) plain (all-purpose) whole-wheat flour*
3 teaspoons baking powder
½ cup (110g) raw sugar
2 tablespoons honey
1 egg
1¼ cups (310ml) buttermilk
⅓ cup (80ml) vegetable oil
1 teaspoon vanilla extract

Preheat oven to 180°C (350°F). Place the flour, baking powder and sugar in a bowl and mix to combine. In a separate bowl, mix to combine the honey, egg, buttermilk, oil and vanilla. Pour the egg mixture into the dry ingredients and mix until just combined.

If using, stir through the fruit and other ingredients.[+] Spoon the mixture into 12 x ½ cup-capacity (125ml) muffin tins lined with paper cases and bake for 25–30 minutes or until cooked when tested with a skewer. Serve warm or cold. MAKES 12
+ See fillings and variations for this recipe on the following pages, 14–15. These muffins will freeze for up to 1 month.

FIVE-GRAIN PORRIDGE

BREAKFAST MUFFINS – *see page 12 for basic muffin recipe*

RASPBERRY *and* OAT
Add 1 cup (160g) fresh or frozen (not thawed) raspberries and ½ cup (45g) rolled oats to the basic mixture. Sprinkle the muffins with extra oats and a little raw sugar before baking.

DATE *and* LSA
Add 1 cup (140g) pitted and chopped soft dates and ⅓ cup LSA* to the basic mixture. Sprinkle with a little raw sugar before baking.

MUESLI
Add ⅓ cup (30g) rolled oats, ¼ cup (35g) chopped dried apricots and ¼ cup (35g) slivered almonds to the basic mixture.

Freeze these MUFFINS *for a quick* BREAKFAST BITE

FIG *and* CINNAMON
Add 1 cup (190g) sliced dried figs and
½ teaspoon ground cinnamon to the basic
mixture. Sprinkle with sugar before baking.

BANANA, BRAN *and* CINNAMON
Add 2 mashed bananas, ⅓ cup (65g) oat
bran* or wheat bran* and 1 teaspoon ground
cinnamon to the basic mixture.

BLUEBERRY *and* APPLE
Add 1 cup (160g) fresh or frozen (not
thawed) blueberries and ⅓ cup (20g)
chopped dried apple to the basic mixture.

QUINOA GRANOLA

QUINOA GRANOLA

1½ cups (300g) white quinoa*
1½ cups (135g) rolled oats
½ cup (70g) sunflower seeds
½ teaspoon ground cinnamon
¼ cup (60ml) maple syrup
2 tablespoons vegetable oil
fresh berries and thick plain yoghurt, to serve

Preheat oven to 180°C (350°F). Place the quinoa, oats, sunflower seeds, cinnamon, maple syrup and oil in a bowl and mix well to combine. Spread the mixture over 2 baking trays lined with non-stick baking paper. Bake for 15 minutes or until golden. Allow to cool. Serve the granola with fresh berries and yoghurt.
SERVES 8–10
+ The granola will keep in an airtight jar for up to 2 weeks.

OVEN-BAKED FRENCH TOAST

4 thick slices wholegrain bread
2 eggs
1 cup (250ml) reduced-fat milk
1 teaspoon vanilla extract
2 tablespoons honey, plus extra, for drizzling
½ teaspoon ground cinnamon
fresh or poached fruit and thick plain yoghurt, to serve

Preheat oven to 200°C (400°F). Place the bread in a large baking dish lined with non-stick baking paper. Place the egg, milk, vanilla, honey and cinnamon in a bowl and whisk to combine. Pour the egg mixture over the bread. Allow to stand for 20 minutes or until most of the egg mixture has been absorbed. Bake for 25 minutes or until the bread is golden. Serve with fruit and yoghurt and drizzle with extra honey. SERVES 4

This is my SUPER-CHARGED version of granola. The addition of quinoa means it's full of protein, which is just the thing to get your morning STARTED. Mixed with sunflower seeds, oats and a kiss of cinnamon, it's toasted to crunchy PERFECTION.

OVEN-BAKED FRENCH TOAST

WHIPPED YOGHURT *and* RICOTTA BREAKFAST PARFAIT

WHIPPED YOGHURT *and* RICOTTA BREAKFAST PARFAIT

1½ cups (300g) reduced-fat ricotta
1½ cups (420g) thick plain yoghurt
1 teaspoon vanilla extract
⅓ cup (80ml) maple syrup
sliced fresh fruit, to serve

Place the ricotta, yoghurt, vanilla and maple syrup in a food processor and process until light and smooth. Spoon into bowls and serve with fresh fruit. SERVES 4

ASPARAGUS, TOMATO *and* FETA EGGWHITE OMELETTE

2 teaspoons vegetable oil
6 spears green asparagus, thinly sliced lengthways with
  a vegetable peeler
6 eggwhites
¼ cup (60ml) water
sea salt and cracked black pepper
2 heirloom tomatoes, cut into wedges
¼ cup mint leaves
100g marinated feta

Heat an 18cm non-stick frying pan over medium heat. Add half the oil and half the asparagus and cook for 2 minutes. Place the eggwhite and water in a bowl and whisk until foamy. Whisk through the salt and pepper. Pour half the eggwhite mixture over the asparagus and cook for 3 minutes. Place the frying pan under a preheated hot grill (broiler) and cook for 2 minutes or until the omelette is set. Remove from the pan and keep warm. Repeat with the remaining oil, asparagus and eggwhite mixture. Fold each omelette in half and serve with the combined tomato and mint and the feta. SERVES 2

This is my chic take on the eggwhite omelette, because LIFE is too short to be bland. Filled with FRESH asparagus, juicy tomato and creamy feta, it makes for a more exciting taste sensation. I prefer it on its own, but you can ENJOY it with toast, too.

ASPARAGUS, TOMATO *and* FETA EGGWHITE OMELETTE

These POWER SMOOTHIES *pack a* REAL PUNCH

SMOOTHIES

MANGO *and* WHEAT GERM
Place 1 cup (200g) chopped mango, ¼ cup (60ml) orange juice, ¼ cup (70g) thick plain yoghurt, ½ cup (125ml) soy milk, 1 tablespoon wheat germ* and 6 ice cubes and in a blender and blend until smooth. SERVES 1

STRAWBERRY *and* SOY
Place 1 cup (250ml) soy or reduced-fat milk, 50g silken tofu*, 6 strawberries, 1 tablespoon honey and 6 ice cubes in a blender and blend until smooth. SERVES 1

MINT, PINEAPPLE, YOGHURT
Place ¾ cup (180ml) reduced-fat milk, ¼ cup (70g) reduced-fat plain yoghurt, ⅓ cup (75g) chopped pineapple, 1 tablespoon honey, 6 ice cubes and 1 tablespoon mint leaves in a blender and blend until smooth. SERVES 1

ALMOND MILK, DATE *and* HONEY
Place 1 cup (250ml) almond milk, 3 pitted dates, 2 teaspoons honey, ¼ cup (70g) reduced-fat plain yoghurt, 6 ice cubes and 1 tablespoon oat bran* in a blender and blend until smooth. SERVES 1

BERRY *and* FLAXSEED
Place ¾ cup (180ml) reduced-fat milk and 1 tablespoon flaxseed* in a blender and blend until smooth. Add ¼ cup (70g) thick plain yoghurt, ⅓ cup (80g) frozen raspberries, 6 ice cubes and 1 tablespoon maple syrup and blend until smooth. SERVES 1

PEANUT BUTTER *and* BANANA
Place 1 cup (250ml) reduced-fat milk, 1 tablespoon crunchy peanut butter, 1 small banana, 1 teaspoon honey , 6 ice cubes and 1 tablespoon oat bran* in a blender and blend until smooth. SERVES 1

HERBED TOFU *and* AVOCADO TOASTS

SPINACH *and* RICOTTA QUESADILLAS

HERBED TOFU *and* AVOCADO TOASTS

150g silken tofu*
1 cup mint leaves
1 cup basil leaves
sea salt and cracked black pepper
8 slices whole-wheat bread, toasted
1 avocado, cut into wedges
200g cherry tomatoes, halved
2 tablespoons lime juice
1 long red chilli, seeds removed and thinly sliced

Place the tofu, half the mint and basil leaves, salt and pepper in
a food processor and process until smooth. Spread the tofu mixture
over the toasts. Top with avocado, tomato and remaining mint and
basil. Combine the lime juice and chilli and spoon over the toasts
to serve. SERVES 4

SPINACH *and* RICOTTA QUESADILLAS

65g baby spinach leaves
1 teaspoon finely grated lemon rind
½ cup (100g) reduced-fat ricotta
¼ cup chopped basil leaves
¼ cup (20g) finely grated parmesan
sea salt and cracked black pepper
2 tomatoes, thinly sliced
8 flour tortillas
vegetable oil, for brushing

Place the spinach in a heatproof bowl, pour over boiling water
and stand for 30 seconds. Drain and squeeze out excess water.
Combine the spinach with the lemon rind, ricotta, basil, parmesan,
salt and pepper. Spread the mixture over the base of 4 tortillas.
Top with the tomato and sandwich with the remaining tortillas.
Brush lightly with oil and cook in a large non-stick frying pan over
low–medium heat for 3–4 minutes each side or until golden and
crisp. Cut into quarters and serve warm. SERVES 4

THE BIG BREAKFAST

8 small Portobello mushrooms, trimmed
¼ cup store-bought basil pesto
4 vine-ripened tomatoes
12 sprigs thyme
120g baby spinach leaves
2 teaspoons finely grated lemon rind
1 cup (200g) reduced-fat ricotta
4 eggs, cooked to your liking[+]
toasted whole-wheat bread, to serve
sea salt and cracked black pepper

Preheat oven to 200°C (400°F). Spread the underside of the
mushrooms with pesto and place in a baking dish lined with non-stick
baking paper. Make some cuts in the tomatoes and push the thyme
sprigs into the cuts. Add to the dish with the mushrooms. Roast for
20 minutes or until the mushrooms and tomatoes are soft.

Place the spinach in a heatproof bowl, pour over boiling water
and stand for 30 seconds. Drain and squeeze out excess water.
Top the spinach with the lemon and ricotta. To serve, divide the
mushrooms, tomatoes, spinach mixture, eggs and toast between
plates and sprinkle with salt and pepper. SERVES 4
+ *You could serve this with poached, fried or scrambled eggs.*

LUNCH *and* SALADS

Take your lunch BEYOND the humble sandwich with these ideas that are big on flavour and full of freshness and CRUNCH. There are poached and grilled meats, grains, VIBRANT vegetables and more to give you the energy you need without sending you into an afternoon lull. Plus, I've included my LIGHT take on some old FAVOURITES for a new and imaginative way to enjoy lunch.

ASIAN CHICKEN SALAD *with* CRISP WONTONS

CHICKEN *and* CUCUMBER SALAD *with* YOGHURT DRESSING

ASIAN CHICKEN SALAD
with CRISP WONTONS

20 store-bought wonton wrappers*
vegetable oil, for brushing
2 x 180g chicken breast fillets, poached (see *basics*, page 182)
1 cup Thai basil leaves
1 cup mint leaves
1 cup coriander (cilantro) leaves
2 cups (160g) shredded white cabbage
2 large red chillies, seeds removed and thinly sliced
asian dressing
1 tablespoon fish sauce*
2 tablespoons lime juice
1 tablespoon caster (superfine) sugar

Preheat oven to 180°C (350°F). Place the wonton wrappers on a baking tray lined with non-stick baking paper. Brush very lightly with oil and bake for 10–12 minutes or until golden. Set aside.

Shred the chicken and place in a bowl with the basil, mint, coriander, cabbage and chilli and toss to combine. Mix together the fish sauce, lime juice and sugar, drizzle over the salad and toss to combine. Serve with the crisp wontons. SERVES 4

CHICKEN *and* CUCUMBER SALAD
with YOGHURT DRESSING

3 x 180g chicken breast fillets, poached (see *basics*, page 182)
2 Lebanese cucumbers, sliced lengthways
2 stalks celery, trimmed and thinly sliced
1 cup flat-leaf parsley leaves
2 tablespoons dill sprigs
2 tablespoons mint leaves
yoghurt dressing
¾ cup (210g) thick plain yoghurt
100g soft feta
2 tablespoons lemon juice
1 tablespoon water
sea salt

To make the yoghurt dressing, place the yoghurt, feta, lemon, water and salt in a food processor and process until smooth.

Slice the chicken and divide between serving plates with the cucumber, celery, parsley, dill and mint. Spoon over the dressing to serve. SERVES 4

RAW BEETROOT SALAD
with GRILLED GOAT'S CHEESE

4 large beetroots, peeled and trimmed
1 carrot, peeled and trimmed
100g baby or small beetroot leaves
300g firm goat's cheese, cut into 8 rounds
vegetable oil, for brushing
horseradish dressing
2 tablespoons white wine vinegar
1 tablespoon olive oil
1 teaspoon freshly grated horseradish*
sea salt and cracked black pepper

To make the horseradish dressing, place the vinegar, oil, horseradish, salt and pepper in a bowl and whisk to combine. Set aside.

Using a mandolin, thinly slice the beetroot and carrot and place in a bowl with the beetroot leaves. Add the dressing and toss gently to coat. Divide the salad between serving plates.

Brush the goat's cheese with a little oil and place on a baking tray lined with non-stick baking paper. Cook under a preheated hot grill (broiler) for 8–10 minutes or until golden. Serve the goat's cheese with the salad. SERVES 4

RAW BEETROOT SALAD *with* GRILLED GOAT'S CHEESE

SUMMER ROLLS

CHICKEN *and* MINT
Top softened rice paper rounds with shredded cooked chicken, mint leaves and shredded cabbage. Fold over the ends and roll to enclose.

CRISPY TOFU
Top softened rice paper rounds with thin, crispy fried tofu pieces, shredded carrot, snow pea (mange tout) sprouts and chopped roasted peanuts. Fold over the ends and roll to enclose.

CHILLI SALMON
Sprinkle salmon pieces with dried chilli flakes and pan-fry until cooked to your liking. Top softened rice paper rounds with shredded cucumber, shredded blanched snow peas (mange tout), coriander (cilantro) leaves and the salmon. Fold over the ends and roll to enclose.

These FRESH ROLLS *make a* LIGHT LUNCH

SNOW PEA *and* CASHEW
Top softened rice paper rounds with blanched shredded snow peas (mange tout), shredded carrot, shredded cucumber, shredded blanched asparagus, coriander (cilantro) leaves, cooked vermicelli rice noodles and chopped roasted cashew nuts. Fold over the ends and roll to enclose.

PRAWN *and* HERB
Top softened rice paper rounds with peeled cooked and cleaned prawns (shrimp), cooked vermicelli rice noodles, coriander (cilantro), mint and basil leaves. Fold over the ends and roll to enclose.

BEEF *and* RADISH
Top softened rice paper rounds with thinly sliced cooked beef, thinly sliced radish, bean sprouts and basil leaves. Fold over the ends and roll to enclose.
+ *Serve any of these rolls with a soy and sesame or chilli and ginger dipping sauce (see basics, page 188).*

CARAMELISED PUMPKIN *and* PEARL BARLEY SALAD

CARAMELISED PUMPKIN
and PEARL BARLEY SALAD

750g butternut pumpkin (squash), sliced
2 tablespoons light agave syrup (nectar)* or honey
2 tablespoons white balsamic vinegar
sea salt and cracked black pepper
1½ cups (300g) pearl barley*, rinsed
4½ cups water
250g baby green beans, trimmed and blanched
200g feta, sliced
1 cup flat-leaf parsley leaves
preserved lemon dressing
1 tablespoon olive oil
2 tablespoons white balsamic vinegar
1 teaspoon finely chopped preserved lemon rind*

Preheat oven to 200°C (400°F). To make the dressing, mix to combine the oil, vinegar and preserved lemon and set aside.

Place the pumpkin on a baking tray lined with non-stick baking paper. Mix together the agave syrup, vinegar, salt and pepper and brush the mixture over the pumpkin. Roast the pumpkin for 25–30 minutes or until golden.

While the pumpkin is roasting, cook the pearl barley. Place the barley and water in a saucepan over medium–high heat, bring to the boil and cook, uncovered, for 15 minutes or until tender. Drain and cool slightly. Place the pumpkin, barley, beans, feta and parsley in a bowl and toss gently to combine. Divide between serving plates and spoon over the dressing to serve. SERVES 4

ROASTED CAULIFLOWER
and CHICKEN SALAD

1kg cauliflower, cut into large florets
12 sprigs tarragon
1 tablespoon shredded lemon rind
12 cloves garlic, unpeeled
2 tablespoons vegetable oil
4 x 180g chicken breast fillets, trimmed
sea salt and cracked black pepper
150g rocket (arugula) leaves
1 quantity lemon buttermilk dressing (see *basics*, page 185)

Preheat oven to 200°C (400°F). Place the cauliflower, tarragon, lemon and garlic in a baking dish lined with non-stick baking paper. Drizzle with oil and roast for 15 minutes. Add the chicken to the dish, sprinkle with salt and pepper and roast for a further 15 minutes or until the chicken is cooked through and the cauliflower is golden.

Slice the chicken and toss with the roasted cauliflower, garlic and rocket. Divide between serving plates and spoon over the lemon buttermilk dressing to serve. SERVES 4

These substantial warm salads are packed with GOODNESS *making for a generous lunch or even a* LIGHT *dinner. Full of fresh herbs, zingy lemon and nutty grains or vegetables, all they need is a light dressing to* BALANCE *out the remaining flavours.*

ROASTED CAULIFLOWER *and* CHICKEN SALAD

SAGE VEAL *with* SHAVED PARSNIP SALAD

SAGE VEAL *with* SHAVED PARSNIP SALAD

4 young parsnips, peeled and trimmed
1 bulb fennel, trimmed
¾ cup flat-leaf parsley leaves
4 x 125g veal cutlets
8 sprigs sage
¾ cup (180ml) buttermilk
sea salt and cracked black pepper

Using a julienne peeler, cut the parsnip into thin strips, discarding the woody core. Place in a bowl. Using a mandolin, finely slice the fennel and add to the parsnip with the parsley and toss to combine. Secure a sprig of sage to both sides of the veal using kitchen string and sprinkle with salt and pepper. Heat a large non-stick frying pan over high heat and cook the veal for 4–5 minutes each side or until cooked to your liking.

Whisk the buttermilk with salt and pepper, pour over the parsnip salad and toss to combine. Serve the salad with the veal. SERVES 4

QUINOA SUSHI ROLLS

1 tablespoon rice wine vinegar*
1 teaspoons caster (superfine) sugar
½ teaspoon sea salt flakes
3 cups cooked white quinoa*, cooled slightly (see *basics*, page 179)
6 sheets toasted nori*
150g sashimi-grade tuna, cut into strips
1 avocado, sliced
1 Lebanese cucumber, thinly sliced
1 carrot, peeled and thinly sliced
8 English spinach leaves, shredded
⅓ cup pickled ginger*
½ cup mint leaves
soy sauce and extra pickled ginger, to serve

Place the vinegar, sugar and salt in a bowl and mix to dissolve the sugar. Pour over the quinoa and mix to combine. Spread ½ cup of quinoa over each sheet of nori.

To make the tuna rolls, divide the tuna, avocado and cucumber between three sheets of nori and roll to enclose the filling.

To make the vegetable rolls, divide the carrot, English spinach, pickled ginger and mint between the remaining three sheets of nori and roll to enclose filling. Slice the rolls into rounds and serve with soy sauce and extra pickled ginger. SERVES 4

In my MODERN *update of the sushi roll, I've substituted the short-grain sushi rice for quinoa. I'm amazed at how well it works, lending the roll a* NUTTY *flavour and texture. These rolls are just the thing to take to work for a quick and* EASY *lunch.*

QUINOA SUSHI ROLLS

WHITE SLAW *with* LEMON POACHED CHICKEN

CRISPY TOFU SALAD

WHITE SLAW *with* LEMON POACHED CHICKEN

2 cups (160g) finely sliced white cabbage
2 parsnips, peeled, cored and shredded using a julienne peeler
1 celeriac (celery root), peeled and shredded using a julienne peeler
2 sticks celery, trimmed and finely sliced
sea salt and cracked black pepper
1 cup (250ml) buttermilk
3 tablespoons lemon juice
3 x 180g lemon poached chicken breast fillets (see *basics*, page 182)

Place the cabbage, parsnip, celeriac, celery, salt and pepper in a bowl and toss to combine. Mix together the buttermilk and lemon, pour over the slaw and toss gently to combine. Divide the slaw between serving plates and serve with thick slices of the lemon poached chicken. SERVES 4

CRISPY TOFU SALAD

500g firm tofu*
1 tablespoon vegetable oil
1 tablespoon sesame seeds
400g broccolini (sprouted broccoli), blanched and sliced
150g snow peas (mange tout), blanched
2 Lebanese cucumbers, thinly sliced
1 tablespoon black sesame seeds
miso dressing
2 tablespoons white miso paste*
2 tablespoons mirin*
1 tablespoon rice wine vinegar*
½ teaspoon sesame oil

Preheat oven to 200°C (400°F). To make the miso dressing, place the miso, mirin, vinegar and sesame oil in a bowl and whisk to combine. Set aside.
   Cut the tofu into thin sticks and pat dry on absorbent paper. Place the tofu on baking trays lined with non-stick baking paper, brush with the oil and sprinkle with sesame seeds. Bake for 25 minutes or until the tofu is crisp and golden.
   Divide the broccolini, snow peas and cucumber between serving plates. Spoon the dressing over the salad, sprinkle with the black sesame seeds and top with the crispy tofu to serve. SERVES 4

BROWN RICE SALAD

3 cups cooked brown rice[+]
2 zucchini (courgette), thinly sliced with a julienne peeler
⅓ cup (45g) toasted halved natural almonds
⅓ cup (55g) currants
60g baby rocket (arugula) leaves
sea salt and cracked black pepper
2 tablespoons lemon juice
2 teaspoons honey
goat's cheese dressing
150g soft goat's cheese
½ cup (140g) thick plain yoghurt
sumac*, for sprinkling

Place the rice, zucchini, almonds, currants, rocket, salt and pepper in a bowl and toss to combine. Mix together the lemon and honey, pour over the salad and toss to combine.
   To make the goat's cheese dressing, place the goat's cheese and yoghurt in a food processor and process until smooth. Divide the salad between serving plates with a large spoonful of the dressing and sprinkle with sumac to serve. SERVES 4
 + 1 cup (200g) uncooked rice yields 3 cups cooked rice.

BROWN RICE SALAD

BRUSCHETTA

CHILLI and GARLIC KALE

Spread the bread slices with store-bought caramelised onion relish. Top with stir-fried kale, garlic and chilli and sprinkle with finely grated parmesan.
+ *Use char-grilled whole-wheat or wholegrain bread slices as the base of these bruschetta.*

CELERIAC REMOULADE and PROSCIUTTO

Combine shredded celeriac (celery root) and flat-leaf parsley leaves with a lemon buttermilk dressing (see *basics*, page 185) and toss to combine. Top the bruschetta with the remoulade and slices of prosciutto.

ROASTED GARLIC and ASPARAGUS

Spread the bread slices with soft roasted garlic and top with steamed asparagus. Spoon over whole-egg mayonnaise combined with lemon juice, or a tofu mayonnaise (see *basics*, page 179).

LEMON RICOTTA, TOMATO *and* BASIL

Combine ricotta with finely grated lemon rind and spread over the bread slices. Top with quartered cherry tomatoes, basil leaves, sea salt and cracked black pepper and drizzle with balsamic glaze.

GOAT'S CURD, BROAD BEAN *and* MINT

Spread the bread slices with soft goat's curd. Top with blanched and peeled broad (fava) beans, mint leaves, a squeeze of lemon and sea salt and cracked black pepper.

ROCKET, SALMON *and* CAPER

Spread the bread slices with reduced-fat cream cheese mixed with chopped dill and cracked black pepper. Top with rocket (arugula) leaves, smoked salmon, crispy fried capers and extra dill sprigs. Serve with a wedge of lemon.

ROASTED BRUSSELS SPROUT *and* PEAR SALAD

ROASTED BRUSSELS SPROUT
and PEAR SALAD

500g Brussels sprouts, trimmed and halved
2 firm brown pears, cut into thick wedges
1 red onion, peeled and cut into wedges
8 sprigs sage
2 tablespoons olive oil
¼ cup (60ml) red wine vinegar
2 tablespoons brown sugar
sea salt and cracked black pepper
150g rocket (arugula) leaves
150g firm goat's cheese, grated

Preheat oven to 200°C (400°F). Place the sprouts, cut-side up, pear, onion and sage on a baking tray lined with non-stick baking paper. Mix together the oil, vinegar and sugar and spoon half the dressing over the vegetable mixture. Sprinkle with salt and pepper and roast for 30–35 minutes or until the sprouts are golden. Divide the sprouts, pear, onion, sage and rocket between serving plates. Sprinkle with the goat's cheese and spoon over the remaining dressing to serve. SERVES 4

WARM PUY LENTIL and
RARE TARRAGON BEEF SALAD

1 cup (200g) puy lentils*
12 baby red and golden beetroots, trimmed and scrubbed
2 tablespoons olive oil
2 tablespoons chopped tarragon leaves
2 teaspoons sea salt flakes
1 teaspoon cracked black pepper
1 x 500g beef eye fillet
1 cup flat-leaf parsley leaves
mustard dressing
1 tablespoon balsamic vinegar
1 tablespoon Dijon mustard
1 tablespoon olive oil

Preheat oven to 200°C (400°F). Place the lentils in a bowl, cover with cold water and soak for 20 minutes. Drain and place the lentils in a small saucepan, cover with boiling water and cook for 20 minutes over high heat or until tender. Drain and keep warm.

Place the beetroot on a baking tray lined with non-stick baking paper, drizzle with the oil and roast for 30 minutes. While the beetroot is cooking, combine the tarragon, salt and pepper and sprinkle over the beef to coat. Heat a non-stick frying pan over high heat. Add the beef and cook for 3–4 minutes each side or until well browned. Add the beef to the tray with the beetroot in the last 10 minutes of cooking time and roast for 10 minutes or until the beef is cooked to your liking. Remove from the oven and set the beef aside to rest.

Place the lentils, beetroot and parsley in a bowl. Mix together the vinegar, mustard and oil, pour over the lentils and toss to combine. Thinly slice the beef, divide between serving plates and top with the lentil salad to serve. SERVES 4

This is one of my favourite salads – I even serve it as an ELEGANT *starter if I have friends coming for dinner. The bitterness of the* CARAMELISED *Brussels sprouts works* BEAUTIFULLY *with the sweetness of the pear, and the goat's cheese adds a salty bite.*

WARM PUY LENTIL *and* RARE TARRAGON BEEF SALAD

TOASTED SPICED CHICKPEA SALAD

TOASTED SPICED CHICKPEA SALAD

1 tablespoon olive oil
1 teaspoon ground cumin
1 teaspoon sweet smoked paprika*
½ teaspoon sea salt flakes
1 teaspoon fennel seeds
2 x 400g cans chickpeas (garbanzos), drained
3 carrots, peeled and shredded using a julienne peeler
1 cup coriander (cilantro) leaves
1 cup mint leaves
200g haloumi*, grated
2 tablespoons lemon juice
1 teaspoon honey
1 tablespoon olive oil, extra

Heat a large non-stick frying pan over high heat. Add the oil, cumin, paprika, salt and fennel seeds and cook for 2 minutes or until fragrant. Add the chickpeas and cook, stirring, for 5 minutes or until the chickpeas are toasted and coated in the spices.

Place the carrot, coriander, mint, haloumi, lemon juice, honey and extra oil in a bowl and toss to combine. Divide between serving plates and top with the chickpeas to serve. SERVES 4

QUINOA TABOULI

3 cups cooked white quinoa*, cooled (see *basics*, page 179)
1½ cups flat-leaf parsley leaves
1 cup roughly chopped mint leaves
¼ cup snipped chives
250g cherry tomatoes, quartered
1 tablespoon finely grated lemon rind
2 tablespoons lemon juice
2 tablespoons olive oil
sea salt and cracked black pepper
marinated feta or yoghurt cheese (see *basics*, page 176) and
    Lebanese flatbread, to serve

Place the cooled quinoa, parsley, mint, chives, tomato and lemon rind in a bowl and toss to combine. Mix together the lemon juice, oil, salt and pepper, pour over the salad and toss to combine. Top with crumbled marinated feta or yoghurt cheese and serve with flatbread. SERVES 4

For a fluffier and more textured version of TABOULI *I've swapped the traditional bulgur wheat for* QUINOA *(my new best friend). It's incredibly versatile and a great alternative to couscous or rice. I love to add it to salads for depth and* SUBSTANCE.

QUINOA TABOULI

FAST DINNERS

These **SPEEDY** meal ideas are quick and easy to get on the table but are not short on taste. They're about using **ROBUST** spices, herbs and vegetables, combined with **FAST** cooking techniques to offer a satisfying weeknight solution. I've thrown in a few of my favourite **SHORTCUTS** too, that show even **MINIMAL** effort can be rewarded with a tasty and wholesome dinner.

TWICE-COOKED QUINOA *with* CHIPOTLE *and* LIME CHICKEN

LEMON *and* GOAT'S CHEESE ROASTED CHICKEN

TWICE-COOKED QUINOA *with* CHIPOTLE *and* LIME CHICKEN

1 dried chipotle chilli*
½ cup (125ml) lime juice (approximately 4 limes)
1 tablespoon honey
3 x 180g poached chicken breast fillets, sliced (see *basics*, page 182)
1½ cups coriander (cilantro) leaves
1½ cups mint leaves
2 green onions (scallions), thinly sliced
2 teaspoons vegetable oil
3 cups cooked white quinoa* (see *basics*, page 179)
1 quantity tofu mayonnaise (see *basics*, page 179)

Place the chilli in a small heatproof bowl and cover with boiling water. Stand for 2 minutes. Drain and shred. Combine the chilli, lime and honey and toss with the chicken, coriander, mint and onion. Heat a large non-stick frying pan over high heat. Add the oil and quinoa and cook, stirring, for 12–15 minutes or until the quinoa is slightly crisp and toasted. Serve with the chipotle and lime chicken and the tofu mayonnaise. SERVES 4

LEMON *and* GOAT'S CHEESE ROASTED CHICKEN

1 small bunch thyme
4 x 180g chicken breast fillets, trimmed
100g goat's cheese, sliced
1 lemon, thinly sliced
cracked black pepper
olive oil, for drizzling

Place the thyme in a baking dish lined with non-stick baking paper. Top with the chicken, goat's cheese and lemon, sprinkle with pepper and drizzle with a little oil. Cook the chicken under a preheated hot grill (broiler) for 12–14 minutes or until cooked through. Serve with steamed greens, if desired. SERVES 4

CHILLI, PEPPER *and* BASIL TOFU STIR-FRY

1 tablespoon vegetable oil
750g firm tofu*, drained and chopped
2 large red chillies, sliced
4 cloves garlic, sliced
1 tablespoon shredded ginger
1 teaspoon cracked black pepper
200g gai larn*, trimmed and chopped into large pieces
¼ cup (60ml) light soy sauce
½ cup (125ml) chicken or vegetable stock
¼ cup (60ml) Chinese cooking wine* (Shaoxing)
1 cup basil leaves
cooked vermicelli rice noodles or steamed brown rice, to serve

Heat a large non-stick frying pan or wok over high heat. Add half the oil and the tofu and cook, turning, for 3–4 minutes or until the tofu is golden. Remove from the pan and set aside. Add the remaining oil, chilli, garlic, ginger and pepper and cook, stirring, for 1–2 minutes. Add the gai larn, soy, stock and wine and cook for a further 2–3 minutes or until the greens are tender. Return the tofu to the pan and cook for 2 minutes or until warmed through. Top with the basil and serve with rice noodles or rice. SERVES 4

CHILLI, PEPPER *and* BASIL TOFU STIR-FRY

BEEF, BROCCOLI *and* BLACK BEAN STIR-FRY

BEEF, BROCCOLI *and* BLACK BEAN STIR-FRY

1 tablespoon vegetable oil
1 x 375g beef eye fillet, sliced
2 long red chillies, thinly sliced
1 tablespoon shredded ginger
2 cloves garlic, thinly sliced
⅔ cup (50g) Chinese black beans*, rinsed
360g broccoli, cut into florets
⅓ cup (60ml) chicken stock
4 green onions (scallions), sliced
⅓ cup Thai basil leaves

Heat a wok or large non-stick frying pan over very high heat. Add the oil and beef and cook, stirring, for 1–2 minutes or until well browned. Add the chilli, ginger, garlic and black beans and cook, stirring, for 2 minutes. Remove from the pan and keep warm. Add the broccoli, stock and onions to the wok and cook for 4 minutes, stirring, or until tender. Return the beef to the pan and toss for 1 minute or until warmed through. Top with the basil to serve. SERVES 4

THAI GREEN CURRY CHICKEN SKEWERS *with* GINGER QUINOA

2 tablespoons Thai green curry paste*
¼ cup (60ml) coconut cream*
4 x 150g chicken breast fillets, sliced
3 cups cooked white quinoa* (see *basics*, page 179)
1 tablespoon finely grated ginger
½ cup chopped coriander (cilantro) leaves
2 green onions (scallions), finely chopped
1 teaspoon sesame oil
lime cheeks, mint and extra coriander (cilantro) leaves, to serve

Place the curry paste and coconut cream in a bowl and mix to combine. Thread the chicken onto skewers and place on a baking tray lined with non-stick baking paper. Spread the curry mixture over the chicken to coat. Cook the skewers under a preheated hot grill (broiler) for 5–7 minutes or until cooked through.

Place the quinoa, ginger, coriander, onion and sesame oil in a bowl and toss to combine. Divide the quinoa between serving plates, top with the chicken and serve with lime, mint and coriander. SERVES 4

I love this stir-fry. It's so TASTY *and full of spicy, salty and garlicky flavours to complement such a strong vegetable. Best of all, it's the twin* POWER *foods of beef and* BROCCOLI *meeting in one dish to create a super-quick, simple dinner.*

THAI GREEN CURRY CHICKEN SKEWERS *with* GINGER QUINOA

RED QUINOA, KALE *and* HALOUMI SALAD

RED QUINOA, KALE *and* HALOUMI SALAD

150g kale, trimmed
2½ cups cooked red quinoa* (see *basics*, page 179)
½ cup flat-leaf parsley leaves
500g haloumi, thinly sliced
olive oil, for brushing
smoky lemon dressing
2 tablespoons lemon juice
1 teaspoon sweet smoked paprika*
1 tablespoon olive oil

Cut the kale into large pieces and place in a heatproof bowl. Pour over boiling water and allow to stand for 5 minutes. Drain and pat dry on absorbent paper. Toss the kale with the quinoa and parsley.

To make the smoky lemon dressing, combine the lemon juice, paprika and oil. Pour over the salad and toss to combine.

Heat a non-stick frying pan over medium–high heat. Brush the haloumi with a little oil and cook for 1–2 minutes each side or until golden. Divide the salad between serving plates and top with the haloumi to serve. SERVES 4

LEMON CHICKEN *with* TOMATO SALAD

4 heirloom tomatoes, thickly sliced
2 large buffalo mozzarella*, torn in half
1 cup mint leaves
3 x 180g lemon poached chicken breast fillets (see *basics*, page 182)
150g rocket (arugula) leaves, shredded
lemon dressing
2 tablespoons finely grated lemon rind
1½ teaspoons caster (superfine) sugar
3 tablespoons lemon juice
2 tablespoons olive oil
sea salt

To make the lemon dressing, combine the lemon rind, sugar, lemon juice, oil and salt. Set aside.

Divide the tomato, mozzarella and mint between serving plates. Slice the chicken and toss with the rocket. Top the tomato with the chicken mixture and spoon over the dressing to serve. SERVES 4

BASIC FRITTATA

4 eggs
2 eggwhites, extra
1¼ cups (310ml) milk
sea salt and cracked black pepper

Place the eggs, extra whites, milk, salt and pepper in a bowl and whisk to combine. Heat an 18cm non-stick ovenproof frying pan over medium heat. Add your filling to the basic mixture if using[+] and cook for 3 minutes or until the base has set. Place under a preheated hot grill (broiler) and cook for 5 minutes or until golden and set. SERVES 4
+ *See fillings and variations on the following pages, 66–67.*

This salad is like SUMMER *on a plate. The zingy lemon, cooling mint and peppery rocket lend freshness, while the lemon-infused chicken gives* SUBSTANCE. *A final burst of* CREAMY *mozzarella over the juicy tomatoes makes this a fresh and vibrant salad.*

LEMON CHICKEN *with* TOMATO SALAD

FRITTATA – *see page 64 for basic frittata recipe*

PUMPKIN *and* CAULIFLOWER
Combine 250g chopped pumpkin, 150g cauliflower florets, 2 teaspoons olive oil and 1 teaspoon dried chilli flakes on a baking tray lined with non-stick baking paper and toss to coat. Bake in a preheated 200°C (400°F) oven for 25 minutes or until soft. Add the vegetables to the pan and pour over the basic frittata mixture. Top with sage leaves and cook as per the basic recipe (page 64).

PEA *and* RICOTTA
Cook 1½ cups (180g) peas and 100g baby spinach leaves in the pan for 3 minutes or until warmed through. Pour over the basic frittata mixture. Top with 150g ricotta and cook as per the basic recipe (page 64). Top the cooked frittata with mint leaves to serve.

BASIL *and* TOMATO
Stir ½ cup shredded basil though the basic frittata mixture and pour into the pan. Add ¼ cup grated haloumi and sprinkle with 2 tablespoons grated parmesan. Cook as per the basic recipe (page 64). Top the cooked frittata with 250g halved mixed cherry tomatoes, an extra ¼ cup shaved haloumi and extra basil leaves to serve.

Frittata is a BLANK *canvas for a* TASTY DINNER

SPICED CARROT

Heat 2 teaspoons of oil in the pan, add 1 teaspoon each ground cumin and dried chilli flakes and cook for 2 minutes. Add 1½ cups grated carrot and cook for 4 minutes or until any moisture has evaporated. Pour over the basic frittata mixture and top with 150g goat's cheese. Cook as per the basic recipe (page 64) and top with coriander (cilantro) leaves to serve.

KALE *and* BACON

Before adding your basic mixture, cook 3 rashers chopped bacon in the pan for 3 minutes. Add 100g shredded kale and cook for 2 minutes or until wilted. Pour over the basic frittata mixture and top with 2 tablespoons finely grated parmesan. Cook as per the basic recipe (page 64).

ZUCCHINI, LEMON *and* FETA

Before adding your basic mixture, cook 1½ cups grated zucchini (courgette) and 2 teaspoons finely grated lemon rind in the pan for 2 minutes until soft. Add 2 teaspoons chopped dill. Pour in the basic frittata mixture, top with 150g crumbled feta and cook as per the basic recipe (page 64).

CHICKEN, CELERY *and* BLACK PEPPER STIR-FRY

LIME *and* CHILLI FISH TACOS

CHICKEN, CELERY *and* BLACK PEPPER STIR-FRY

1 tablespoon vegetable oil
1 teaspoon roughly cracked black pepper
½ teaspoon dried chilli flakes
½ teaspoon sea salt flakes
1 white onion, thickly sliced
3 x 180g chicken breast fillets, trimmed and thinly sliced
3 stalks celery, trimmed and thickly sliced
coriander (cilantro) leaves and lime cheeks, to serve

Heat a large non-stick frying pan or wok over high heat. Add the oil, pepper, chilli and salt and cook, stirring, for 2 minutes. Add the onion and cook for 5 minutes. Add the chicken and cook, stirring, for 5 minutes or until the chicken is well browned. Add the celery and cook for a further 2 minutes. Divide between serving plates and serve with the lime, coriander and rice noodles, if desired. SERVES 4

LIME *and* CHILLI FISH TACOS

½ teaspoon dried chilli flakes
1 tablespoon lime juice
1 tablespoon vegetable oil
sea salt and cracked black pepper
8 x 80g pieces firm white fish fillets, skin on
8 butter lettuce leaves
8 tortillas, warmed
1 quantity lime and coriander tofu mayonnaise (see *basics*, page 179)
lime wedges, sliced pickled jalapeño chillies and coriander (cilantro) leaves, to serve

Combine the chilli flakes, lime juice, oil, salt and pepper. Coat both sides of the fish with the mixture. Heat a large non-stick frying pan over high heat. Cook the fish, in batches, for 1–2 minutes each side or until cooked through. Divide the lettuce between the tortillas and top with the fish. Serve with the lime and coriander mayonnaise, lime wedges, jalapeños and coriander. SERVES 4

QUINOA MINESTRONE SOUP *with* ROCKET PESTO

2 teaspoons vegetable oil
2 leeks, trimmed and chopped
2 tablespoons oregano leaves
2 small parsnips, peeled, cored and chopped
1 bulb fennel, finely chopped
300g pumpkin or sweet potato (kumara), peeled and chopped
250g green beans, trimmed and chopped
2 cups (400g) red quinoa*
2 litres chicken or vegetable stock
2 cups (560g) tomato purée (passata)
rocket pesto
50g rocket (arugula) leaves, finely chopped
1 clove garlic, crushed
2 tablespoons pine nuts, chopped
1 tablespoon grated parmesan
1 tablespoon finely grated lemon rind
1 tablespoon lemon juice
1 tablespoon olive oil

Heat a saucepan over medium–high heat. Add the oil, leek and oregano and cook for 5 minutes or until soft. Add the parsnip, fennel, pumpkin, beans, quinoa, stock and tomato purée and bring to the boil. Reduce heat to a simmer, cover, and cook for 8–10 minutes or until the vegetables and quinoa are tender.

To make the rocket pesto, combine the rocket, garlic, pine nuts, parmesan, lemon rind and juice and olive oil. Divide the soup between bowls and top with the rocket pesto to serve. SERVES 4

QUINOA MINESTRONE SOUP *with* ROCKET PESTO

GINGER POACHED CHICKEN *with* FENNEL *and* APPLE SLAW

GINGER POACHED CHICKEN
with FENNEL *and* APPLE SLAW

2 cups (500ml) chicken stock
8 slices ginger
2 cloves garlic, sliced
3 x 180g chicken breast fillets, trimmed
1 tablespoon sesame seeds, toasted
sea salt
fennel and apple slaw
2 bulbs baby fennel, thinly sliced on a mandolin
1 Granny Smith apple, thinly sliced on a mandolin
1 cup mint leaves
¾ cup (180ml) buttermilk
2 tablespoons lemon juice

Place the stock, ginger and garlic in a deep frying pan over medium heat and bring to a simmer. Add the chicken and cook for 5 minutes each side. Remove the pan from the heat and allow the chicken to stand for 10 minutes. Remove the chicken from the stock, shred and toss with the sesame seeds and salt.

To make the fennel and apple slaw, combine the fennel, apple and mint. Divide between serving plates and top with the shredded chicken. Combine the buttermilk and lemon juice and spoon over the salad to serve. SERVES 4

GINGER *and* LEMONGRASS
GRILLED CHICKEN

1 tablespoon grated ginger
2 stalks lemongrass*, white part only, very finely chopped
2 tablespoons chopped coriander (cilantro) leaves
1 tablespoon vegetable oil
sea salt and cracked black pepper
4 x 180g chicken breast fillets, trimmed and halved lengthways
2 Lebanese cucumbers, thickly sliced lengthways
½ red onion, finely sliced
1½ cups coriander (cilantro) leaves, extra
1½ cups mint leaves
kecap manis* (sweet soy sauce) and lime cheeks, to serve

Combine the ginger, lemongrass, coriander, oil, salt and pepper. Spread the mixture over the chicken and allow to marinate for 10 minutes. Heat a non-stick char-grill pan or barbecue over high heat and cook the chicken for 2–3 minutes each side or until just cooked through.

Divide the cucumber, onion, coriander and mint between serving plates. Top with the chicken, drizzle with kecap manis and serve with the lime. SERVES 4

The elements in this salad are a match made in HEAVEN. *Crunchy sweet apple and bitter fennel make the* PERFECT *partners, while tangy lemon and creamy buttermilk provide a lovely contrast. A kiss of ginger in the chicken pulls it all* TOGETHER.

GINGER *and* LEMONGRASS GRILLED CHICKEN

ESSENTIAL GREEN SOUP

ESSENTIAL GREEN SOUP

2 teaspoons olive oil
1 leek, trimmed and sliced
2 cloves garlic, sliced
400g broccoli, chopped
150g kale, roughly chopped
100g English spinach, roughly chopped
100g silver beet or Swiss chard, roughly chopped
2 litres chicken or vegetable stock
2 teaspoons grated lemon rind
sea salt and cracked black pepper
300g silken tofu*

Heat a large saucepan over high heat. Add the oil, leek and garlic and cook for 5 minutes or until very soft. Add the broccoli, kale, spinach, silverbeet and stock. Bring to the boil, reduce heat, cover and cook for 5 minutes or until the vegetables are just tender. Stir through the lemon rind, salt and pepper. Using a stick blender or a blender, purée the soup until smooth. Add the tofu and blend until smooth. SERVES 4

PRESERVED LEMON CHICKEN *with* KALE

1 tablespoon vegetable oil
2 tablespoons shredded preserved lemon rind*
3 cloves garlic, crushed
¼ cup (35g) slivered almonds
3 cups cooked brown rice+
3 x 180g chicken breast fillets, trimmed and thinly sliced
200g kale, trimmed and roughly chopped

Combine the oil, lemon rind and garlic. Heat a deep frying pan over high heat. Add half the lemon mixture and the almonds and cook for 3 minutes or until the almonds are golden. Add the rice and cook, stirring, for 5–7 minutes or until warmed through and slightly crisp. Remove from the pan and set aside.

Wipe the pan clean and heat over high heat. Add the remaining lemon mixture and the chicken and cook, stirring, for 3–4 minutes or until the chicken is well browned. Add the kale and cook, stirring, for 2–3 minutes. Return the rice to the pan and cook, stirring, for 3 minutes or until warmed through. Divide between plates to serve. SERVES 4
+ 1 cup (200g) uncooked rice yields 3 cups cooked rice.

Robust kale needs a STRONG *flavour to complement it, which is why the salty tang of preserved lemon is ideal, as well as the toasted nuttiness of the* ALMONDS. *You could eat this dish as a* WARM *salad and it's the ideal leftover for lunch at the office.*

PRESERVED LEMON CHICKEN *with* KALE

NO-COOK PASTA SAUCE

MINT, LEMON *and* FETA
Combine 1 cup mint leaves,
2 shredded zucchinis (courgettes),
2 teaspoons finely grated lemon rind,
⅓ cup (80ml) lemon juice, 2 teaspoons
olive oil, 100g crumbled feta, salt and
pepper. Toss through 200g hot spaghetti
to serve. SERVES 2

GREEN OLIVE *and*
TOASTED ALMOND
Combine ½ cup (80g) sliced green olives,
¼ cup (35g) toasted slivered almonds,
50g shredded baby rocket (arugula) leaves,
2 tablespoons each lemon juice and olive oil,
finely grated parmesan, salt and pepper.
Toss through 200g hot spaghetti to serve.
SERVES 2

DOUBLE TOMATO *and* BASIL
Combine ⅓ cup finely chopped sun-dried
tomatoes, 250g quartered mixed cherry
tomatoes, 1 cup basil leaves, 1 tablespoon
each white balsamic vinegar and olive oil,
sea salt, cracked black pepper and finely
grated parmesan. Toss through 200g hot
spaghetti to serve. SERVES 2

These NO-COOK *sauces are* FAST AND FRESH

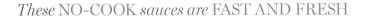

SMOKED TROUT *and* RICOTTA
Combine 300g flaked smoked trout, ½ cup flat-leaf parsley leaves, 1 tablespoon each finely grated lemon rind and lemon juice, 2 tablespoons olive oil, salt and pepper. Toss with 200g hot spaghetti and top with 1 cup (200g) crumbled ricotta to serve.
SERVES 2

BROCCOLI PESTO
Place 300g blanched broccoli, 1 clove crushed garlic, ½ cup flat-leaf parsley leaves, ⅓ cup (50g) pine nuts and 2 tablespoons olive oil in a food processor and process until finely chopped. Toss through 200g hot spaghetti and sprinkle with finely grated parmesan, salt and pepper. SERVES 2

TUNA, CHILLI, ROCKET *and* LEMON
Combine 1 x 185g can drained tuna, 1 chopped long red chilli, 1 bunch torn rocket (arugula) leaves, ¼ cup (60ml) lemon juice, 1 tablespoon olive oil and 2 tablespoons rinsed capers. Toss through 200g hot spaghetti to serve. SERVES 2

OVEN-BAKED BEANS

FENNEL *and* ORANGE CHICKEN SKEWERS *with* CARROT SALAD

OVEN-BAKED BEANS

8 cloves garlic, peeled
750g truss cherry tomatoes
100g flat pancetta*, chopped
6 sprigs oregano
2 x 400g cans butter or large lima beans, drained and rinsed
½ cup (125ml) vegetable or chicken stock
grated parmesan and char-grilled sourdough bread, to serve

Preheat oven to 200°C (400°F). Place the garlic, tomato, pancetta and oregano in a baking dish and bake for 30 minutes. Add the beans and stock and cook for a further 10 minutes or until the beans are warmed through. Sprinkle the beans with parmesan and serve with the bread and wilted baby spinach, if desired. SERVES 4

FENNEL *and* ORANGE CHICKEN SKEWERS *with* CARROT SALAD

¼ cup (60ml) orange juice
1 tablespoon honey
1 teaspoon fennel seeds, toasted
1 tablespoon vegetable oil
1 tablespoon lemon juice
1 clove garlic, crushed
750g chicken thigh fillets, trimmed and sliced
12 baby rainbow carrots, thinly sliced with a vegetable peeler

Place the orange juice, honey, fennel, oil, lemon juice and garlic in a bowl. Place the chicken in a separate bowl, pour over half the orange juice mixture and allow to marinate in the fridge for 20 minutes. Thread the chicken onto skewers. Place the chicken on a baking tray lined with non-stick baking paper and cook under a hot preheated grill (broiler) and for 2 minutes each side, basting with the marinade, or until the chicken is cooked through.
   Toss the carrot with the remaining orange mixture, divide between serving plates and top with the chicken to serve. SERVES 4

PRESERVED LEMON CHICKEN SOUP

1.5 litres chicken stock
1 tablespoon finely shredded preserved lemon rind*
2 x 180g chicken breast fillets, trimmed
1 stalk celery, trimmed and chopped
1 zucchini (courgette), chopped
6 spears asparagus, thinly sliced with a vegetable peeler
1½ cups cooked risoni or short pasta
2 teaspoons thyme leaves
2 green onions (scallions), sliced
sea salt and cracked black pepper

Place the stock and lemon rind in a saucepan over medium–high heat and bring to the boil. Add the chicken, cover and cook for 5 minutes or until just cooked through. Remove the chicken from the stock, shred and set aside.
   Add the celery and zucchini to the pan and cook for 3 minutes. Add the asparagus and cook for 1 minute. Return the chicken to the pan with the risoni, thyme, onion, salt and pepper and cook until warmed through. SERVES 4

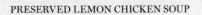

PRESERVED LEMON CHICKEN SOUP

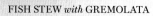

FISH STEW *with* GREMOLATA

CHICKEN *and* SPINACH PATTIES

CHICKEN *and* SPINACH PATTIES

200g English spinach, trimmed
1 thick slice fresh bread
1 x 180g chicken breast fillet, trimmed and chopped
375g chicken thigh fillets, trimmed and chopped
1 eggwhite
sea salt and cracked black pepper
½ cup flat-leaf parsley leaves, chopped
100g feta, chopped
2 green onions (scallions), chopped
⅓ cup (50g) sesame seeds
vegetable oil, for brushing
lemon wedges and lime and tofu mayonnaise (see *basics*, page 179),
    to serve

Preheat oven to 180°C (350°F). Place the spinach in a heatproof bowl and pour over boiling water. Allow to stand for 1 minute, drain and squeeze out remaining moisture. Roughly chop the spinach and set aside.

   Place the bread in a food processor and process to form large breadcrumbs. Add the chicken, eggwhite, salt and pepper and pulse until finely chopped and combined. Transfer to a bowl and add the spinach, parsley, feta and onion and mix to combine. Shape ⅓ cupfuls of the mixture into patties and press both sides into the sesame seeds. Brush the patties lightly with oil. Heat a large non-stick frying pan over medium heat. Cook the patties for 3 minutes each side or until golden. Transfer to a baking tray lined with non-stick baking paper and bake for 8 minutes or until cooked through. Serve with the lemon, mayonnaise and a simple tomato and basil salad, if desired. MAKES 10

FISH STEW *with* GREMOLATA

1 teaspoon olive oil
4 eschalots (French shallots), peeled and thinly sliced
2 cloves garlic, sliced
1 teaspoon dried chilli flakes
750ml fish stock
1 x 400g can cherry tomatoes
750g firm white fish fillets, skin off, cut into large cubes
16 clams (vongole), cleaned
sea salt and cracked black pepper
½ cup flat-leaf parsley laves
1 tablespoon finely grated lemon rind

Heat a deep frying pan over medium–high heat. Add the oil, eschalots, garlic and chilli and cook for 2 minutes or until soft. Add the stock and tomatoes and simmer for 10 minutes. Add the fish, clams, salt and pepper and cook for 5 minutes or until cooked through and the clams have opened. Divide the soup between bowls and top with the parsley and lemon rind to serve. SERVES 4

MISO COD *with* EDAMAME

2 tablespoons salt-reduced soy sauce
1 tablespoon honey
1 tablespoon white miso paste*
1 tablespoon finely grated ginger
4 x 150g cod fillets, skin off
2 Lebanese cucumbers, thinly sliced lengthways
180g shelled edamame (baby soy beans), blanched
4 green onions (scallions), finely sliced
miso dressing
2 tablespoons white miso paste*
¼ cup (60ml) mirin*
2 teaspoons finely grated ginger
1 teaspoon sesame oil

To make the miso dressing, place the miso, mirin, ginger and sesame oil in a bowl and whisk to combine. Set aside.

   Combine the soy, honey, miso and ginger and pour over the fish. Allow to marinate in the fridge for 10 minutes each side. Heat a large non-stick frying pan over high heat. Add the fish and cook for 3 minutes each side or until the fish is slightly blackened on the outside and cooked to your liking.

   Divide the cucumber, edamame and green onion between serving plates. Top with the fish and pour over the miso dressing to serve. SERVES 4

MISO COD *with* EDAMAME

SPINACH *and* RICOTTA GNOCCHI

LENTIL FALAFEL *with* GARLIC YOGHURT SAUCE

QUINOA ROASTED CHICKEN
with OLIVE GREMOLATA

1½ cups (300g) white quinoa*
2⅔ cups (660ml) chicken stock
150g green beans, trimmed
4 x 150g chicken breast fillets, trimmed
sea salt and cracked black pepper
olive gremolata
1½ cups roughly chopped flat-leaf parsley leaves
1 cup roughly chopped mint leaves
1 tablespoon finely grated lemon rind
2 tablespoons lemon juice
½ cup (80g) chopped black olives
1 tablespoon olive oil

Preheat oven to 180°C (350°F). Place the quinoa in the base of an oven-proof baking dish. Heat the stock in a saucepan until boiling and pour over the quinoa. Cover and bake for 10 minutes. Stir the quinoa and top with the beans and chicken. Sprinkle with salt and pepper and cover the dish tightly with aluminium foil. Bake for 25–30 minutes or until the quinoa is tender and the chicken is cooked through.

While the chicken is cooking, make the olive gremolata. Mix to combine the parsley, mint, lemon rind and juice, olives and oil. Divide the chicken and quinoa between serving plates and spoon over the olive gremolata to serve. SERVES 4

SPINACH *and* RICOTTA GNOCCHI

450g frozen spinach, thawed
1½ cups (300g) ricotta
½ cup (40g) finely grated parmesan
1 tablespoon finely grated lemon rind
1¼ cups (190g) plain (all-purpose) flour
2 eggs
4–6 heirloom tomatoes, sliced
½ cup basil leaves
sea salt and cracked black pepper
olive oil and finely grated parmesan, to serve

Squeeze the excess moisture from the spinach and place in a bowl with the ricotta, parmesan, lemon, flour and eggs. Mix well to form a soft dough. Place on a lightly floured surface and divide the dough into 2 pieces. Roll each piece into a 40cm long rope and cut into 3cm pieces. Place on a lightly floured tray until ready to cook.

Cook the gnocchi in a large saucepan of boiling salted water for 5 minutes or until cooked through. Divide the tomato and gnocchi between serving plates, top with the basil and sprinkle with salt and pepper. Drizzle with a little olive oil and sprinkle with parmesan to serve. SERVES 4

LENTIL FALAFEL *with*
GARLIC YOGHURT SAUCE

1 x 400g can brown lentils, drained and rinsed
1 cup (70g) fresh breadcrumbs
100g ricotta
1 egg
1 teaspoon ground cumin
½ cup coriander (cilantro) leaves
1 teaspoon finely grated lemon rind
sea salt and cracked black pepper
vegetable oil, for brushing
salad greens and mustard cress*, to serve
garlic yoghurt sauce
1 cup (280g) thick plain yoghurt
2 cloves garlic, crushed
2 tablespoons tahini paste*
2 tablespoons lemon juice
2 tablespoons chopped chives

Preheat oven to 220°C (450°F). To make the garlic yoghurt sauce, combine the yoghurt, garlic, tahini, lemon juice and chives. Set aside.

Place the lentils, breadcrumbs, ricotta, egg, cumin, coriander, lemon, salt and pepper in a food processor and pulse until the mixture is just combined. Shape 2 tablespoonsful of the mixture into small patties and place on a baking tray lined with non-stick baking paper. Brush the patties lightly with oil and bake for 10 minutes each side or until crisp. Divide the falafels between serving plates with the salad greens and cress and serve with the garlic yoghurt sauce. SERVES 4

QUINOA ROASTED CHICKEN *with* OLIVE GREMOLATA

GRILLED LAMB *and* EGGPLANT *with* FETA *and* MINT

GRILLED LAMB *and* EGGPLANT *with* FETA *and* MINT

2 tablespoons olive oil
2 tablespoons red wine vinegar
2 tablespoons chopped oregano
sea salt and cracked black pepper
550g lamb backstraps (boneless loin)
2 small eggplants (aubergines), sliced lengthways
1½ cups mint leaves
½ cup dill sprigs
150g firm feta, crumbled
1 tablespoon lemon juice
1 teaspoon honey

Combine the oil, vinegar, oregano, salt and pepper and brush over the lamb and eggplant. Cook on a hot char-grill pan or barbecue for 3–4 minutes each side or until the eggplant is dark golden and tender and the lamb is cooked to your liking.

Thickly slice the lamb and divide between serving plates with the eggplant. Top with the mint, dill and feta. Combine the lemon juice and honey and spoon over the lamb to serve. SERVES 4

SPICY CHICKEN LARB *with* PICKLED CUCUMBER

500g chicken mince (ground chicken)
2 tablespoons grated ginger
3 cloves garlic, crushed
¼ cup chilli jam*
1 tablespoon vegetable oil
1 tablespoon fish sauce*
2 tablespoons lime juice
coriander (cilantro) leaves and butter lettuce leaves, to serve
pickled cucumber
2 tablespoons rice wine vinegar*
1 clove garlic, crushed
2 teaspoons caster (superfine) sugar
2 Lebanese cucumbers, thinly sliced using a vegetable peeler
1 long red chilli, sliced

To make the pickled cucumber, place the vinegar, garlic and sugar in a bowl and stir to dissolve the sugar. Add the cucumber and chilli and allow to stand for 10 minutes.

Place the chicken, ginger, garlic and chilli jam in a bowl and mix to combine. Heat the oil in a wok or non-stick frying pan over high heat. Add the chicken mixture and cook, stirring, for 5 minutes or until the chicken is well browned. Add the fish sauce and lime juice and cook for a further 3–4 minutes or until the chicken is cooked through. Divide the chicken between bowls, top with the coriander and serve with the lettuce leaves and pickled cucumber. SERVES 4

This is my combination of CLASSIC *Mediterranean ingredients with a lighter touch. The charry flavour of the barbecued lamb and eggplant gives a lovely* SMOKY *finish, while salty feta,* COOLING *mint and a tangy-sweet honey dressing complete the dish.*

SPICY CHICKEN LARB *with* PICKLED CUCUMBER

QUINOA PEA FRITTERS *with* ZUCCHINI

QUINOA PEA FRITTERS *with* ZUCCHINI

2 cups (240g) cooked peas
2 cups cooked white quinoa* (see *basics*, page 179)
1 eggwhite
2 tablespoons rice flour*
2 tablespoons vegetable oil
sea salt and cracked black pepper
2 teaspoons vegetable oil, extra
2 zucchinis (courgettes), shredded using a julienne peeler
1 tablespoon lemon juice
½ cup mint leaves
⅔ cup yoghurt cheese, (see *basics*, page 176)
lemon cheeks, to serve

Roughly mash half the peas and place in a bowl with the quinoa, eggwhite, rice flour, oil, salt and pepper and mix well to combine. Shape ¼ cupfuls of the mixture into thin patties. Heat the extra oil in a large non-stick frying pan over medium heat and cook, in batches, for 3–4 minutes each side until golden. Drain on absorbent paper. Toss the remaining peas with the zucchini, lemon and mint and serve with the fritters, yoghurt cheese and lemon cheeks.
SERVES 4

QUINOA CRUST PUMPKIN PIE

1½ cups cooked white quinoa* (see *basics*, page 179)
1 eggwhite
sea salt and cracked black pepper
roasted pumpkin filling
1kg butternut pumpkin (squash), peeled and chopped
2 small zucchinis (courgettes), chopped
8 sprigs sage
sea salt and cracked black pepper
1 tablespoon vegetable oil
150g firm feta, sliced

Preheat oven to 200°C (400°F). To make the roasted pumpkin filling, toss together the pumpkin, zucchini, sage, salt, pepper and oil and place on a baking tray. Roast for 25 minutes or until the pumpkin is soft. Set aside.

Reduce heat to 160°C (325°F). Place the quinoa, eggwhite, salt and pepper in a bowl and mix well to combine. Press the mixture into a 20cm greased pie dish using the back of a spoon. Bake the pie shell for 30 minutes or until slightly crisp. Fill the pie shell with the pumpkin mixture and top with the feta. Bake for 15 minutes or until the vegetables are warmed through and the feta is golden. Serve warm in wedges. SERVES 4

This is my TRICK *to creating a crispy pie crust without using lots of butter and flour. It's another great example of quinoa's* VERSATILITY *in the kitchen – I've also used it in these* TASTY *golden fritters, which I'm just as happy to munch on cold for lunch!*

QUINOA CRUST PUMPKIN PIE

PAPER PARCELS

FISH *with* XO SAUCE

Place a halved bok choy on sheets of non-stick baking paper. Top with a firm white fish fillet. Sprinkle with lemon juice and sesame oil. Fold over the ends of the paper to enclose the filling, place on a baking tray and bake in a 200°C (400°F) oven for 12–15 minutes. Spoon over XO sauce* to serve.

GARLIC PRAWNS

Place trimmed mixed beans on sheets of non-stick baking paper. Top with peeled green (raw) prawns. Sprinkle with chopped red chilli, crushed garlic and drizzle with oil. Fold over the ends of the paper to enclose the filling and place on a baking tray. Bake in a 200°C (400°F) oven for 12–15 minutes. Top with flat-leaf parsley to serve.

SPICED CHICKEN

Place shredded sweet potato on sheets of non-stick baking paper. Top with a chicken breast and sprinkle with za'atar* and a little vegetable oil. Fold over the ends of the paper to enclose the filling and place on a baking tray. Bake in a 200°C (400°F) oven for 12–15 minutes. Serve with thick plain yoghurt and mint leaves.

COCONUT *and* LIME SALMON
Place ½ cup cooked brown rice on sheets of non-stick baking paper. Top with a salmon fillet, sprinkle with shredded chilli and kaffir lime and drizzle with coconut milk. Fold over the ends of the paper to enclose the filling and place on a baking tray. Bake in a 200°C (400°F) oven for 12–15 minutes. Serve with coriander (cilantro) and mint leaves.

CHILLI JAM TOFU
Place trimmed snake beans on sheets of non-stick baking paper. Top with thick slices of firm tofu and spoon over chilli jam*. Fold over the ends of the paper to enclose the filling and place on a baking tray. Bake in a 200°C (400°F) oven for 12–15 minutes. Top with sliced red chilli and green onions (scallions) to serve.

MOROCCAN MUSSELS
Place ½ cup cooked couscous on sheets of non-stick baking paper. Top with mussels and a few spoonfuls of chermoula* and drizzle with coconut milk. Fold over the ends of the paper to enclose the filling and place on a baking tray. Bake in a 200°C (400°F) oven for 12–15 minutes. Serve with coriander (cilantro) leaves.

SILVER BEET *and* RICOTTA TART

QUINOA *and* CHICKPEA BURGERS

SILVER BEET *and* RICOTTA TART

1¼ cups (190g) plain (all-purpose) whole-wheat flour*
sea salt and cracked black pepper
40g unsalted butter, chopped
150g reduced-fat cream cheese, chopped
1 egg yolk
filling
4 stalks silver beet* (Swiss chard), stalks removed and sliced
2 eggs
450g ricotta
½ cup (125ml) milk
1 teaspoon finely grated lemon rind
¼ cup chopped flat-leaf parsley leaves
1 cup (125g) grated gruyère*
6 small sprigs oregano

Preheat oven to 190°C (375°F). Place the flour, salt, pepper and butter in a food processor and process until well combined. Add the cream cheese and egg yolk and process until a soft dough forms. Roll the dough out on a lightly floured surface to 3mm thick and use it to line a 24cm springform tin. Top the pastry with non-stick baking paper and fill with baking weights or dried beans. Blind bake for 15 minutes, remove the weights or beans and bake for a further 5 minutes or until the pastry is crisp. Set aside.

To make the filling, place the silver beet in a heatproof bowl and pour over boiling water to cover. Stand for 3 minutes, drain and pat dry on absorbent paper. Place the silverbeet in the base of the pastry shell.

Place the egg, ricotta, milk, lemon and parsley in a bowl and whisk to combine. Pour over the silver beet and top with the gruyère and oregano. Bake for 35 minutes or until the filling is set. Serve warm with salad greens, if desired. SERVES 6

QUINOA *and* CHICKPEA BURGERS

½ cup (100g) white quinoa*
1 cup (250ml) vegetable stock
2 small slices whole-wheat bread
1 x 400g can chickpeas (garbanzos), drained and rinsed
1 egg
¼ cup coriander (cilantro) leaves
1 teaspoon ground cumin
1 small red chilli, chopped
sea salt and cracked black pepper
vegetable oil, for brushing
4 small flatbreads
salad greens, sliced avocado and tomato, to serve
lime and coriander tofu mayonnaise, to serve (see *basics*, page 179)

Place the quinoa and stock in a saucepan and bring to the boil. Cover, reduce heat to low and cook for 15 minutes or until all the stock has been absorbed. Set aside and cool slightly.

Place the bread in a food processor and process until fine breadcrumbs form. Add the chickpeas, quinoa, egg, coriander, cumin, chilli, salt and pepper and process in short bursts until the mixture is finely chopped. Shape the mixture into 4 patties. Brush the patties with oil and cook in a non-stick frying pan over medium–high heat for 4 minutes each side or until golden. Divide the flatbread between serving plates and top with the lettuce, pattie, avocado and tomato and spoon over the mayonnaise to serve. SERVES 4

BARLEY RISOTTO

2 teaspoons olive oil
150g speck*, chopped
2 leeks, trimmed and sliced
2 cloves garlic, thinly sliced
4 sprigs thyme
1½ cups (300g) pearl barley*
½ cup (125ml) red wine
1.25 litres chicken stock
100g cavalo nero (Tuscan cabbage), shredded
finely grated parmesan, to serve

Heat the oil in a large saucepan over medium–high heat. Add the speck and cook for 5 minutes or until golden. Add the leek and cook for 5 minutes or until soft and golden. Add the garlic, thyme and barley and cook for 2 minutes. Add the wine and cook for 2 minutes or until the wine has been absorbed. Add the stock and bring to the boil. Reduce heat to low, cover and cook for 20–25 minutes or until the barley is soft and the stock has been absorbed. Stir through the cavalo nero and cook for 3 minutes or until tender. Divide the risotto between bowls and top with the parmesan to serve. SERVES 4

BARLEY RISOTTO

INDIVIDUAL MOUSSAKA

INDIVIDUAL MOUSSAKA

8 large (1cm thick) slices eggplant (aubergine)
500g lamb mince (ground lamb)
2 cloves garlic, crushed
1 tablespoon oregano leaves
2 small zucchinis (courgettes), grated
150g feta, crumbled
1 cup (70g) fresh breadcrumbs
1 tablespoon honey
sea salt and cracked black pepper
1 tablespoon olive oil
1¼ cups (250g) ricotta
1 cup (100g) grated mozzarella
1 tablespoon oregano leaves, extra

Preheat oven to 180°C (350°F). Place half the eggplant slices in a baking dish lined with non-stick baking paper. Place the lamb, garlic, oregano, zucchini, feta, breadcrumbs, honey, salt and pepper in a bowl and mix to combine. Divide the mixture into 4 and press on top of half the eggplant slices. Top with the remaining eggplant slices. Brush with the oil, top with ricotta and mozzarella and sprinkle with oregano leaves. Bake for 50 minutes or until the lamb is cooked through and the cheese is golden. Serve with a simple green salad, if desired. SERVES 4

GRILLED STEAK *with* GREEN SALSA

2 teaspoons smoked paprika*
sea salt and cracked black pepper
4 x 150g rump steaks, trimmed
4 zucchinis (courgettes), thickly sliced lengthways
vegetable oil, for brushing
crispy potato fries, to serve (see *snacks and sides*, page 122)
green salsa
½ cup coriander (cilantro) leaves
½ cup flat-leaf parsley leaves
1 clove garlic, crushed
1 large green chilli, seeds removed
2 tablespoons malt or cider vinegar*
1 teaspoon white sugar
1 tablespoon olive oil

To make the green salsa, place the coriander, parsley, garlic, chilli, vinegar, sugar and oil in a food processor or blender and process until finely chopped. Set aside.

Mix together the paprika, salt and pepper and sprinkle over both sides of the steaks. Heat a char-grill pan or barbecue over high heat. Cook the steaks for 2 minutes each side or until cooked to your liking. Set aside to rest.

Brush the zucchini with a little oil and char-grill or barbecue for 2 minutes each side or until just tender. Divide the zucchini between serving plates. Slice the steak and place over the zucchini. Spoon over the green salsa and serve with the crispy potato fries. SERVES 4

This is my version of Greek MOUSSAKA, *made miniature. These individual serves come without the heavy bechamel sauce, and a* COMBINATION *of feta, ricotta and mozzarella lends a molten cheesy flavour, while the lamb adds a* ROBUST *depth.*

GRILLED STEAK *with* GREEN SALSA

CRISPY-SKIN SALMON *with* CHILLI BROTH

CRISPY-SKIN SALMON *with* CHILLI BROTH

8 x 90g salmon fillets, skin on
vegetable oil, for brushing
sea salt
2 limes, halved
crispy fried shredded ginger, to serve
chilli broth
2 cups (500ml) fish stock
2 small green chillies, sliced
3 kaffir lime leaves*, shredded
1 tablespoon white miso paste*
250g broccoli, sliced

To make the chilli broth, place the stock, chilli, lime leaf and miso
in a saucepan over medium heat. Cover and simmer for 5 minutes
or until the flavours have infused. Add the broccoli and cook for
2 minutes. Set aside.

Brush the salmon skin with a little oil and sprinkle with salt.
Heat a non-stick frying pan over high heat, add the salmon,
skin-side down, and cook for 2 minutes each side. Add the limes
to the pan, cut-side down, and cook until caramelised.

Divide the chilli broth and broccoli between bowls and top with
the salmon. Serve with the caramelised limes and fried ginger.
SERVES 4

WHOLE-WHEAT PIZZA BASE

2 cups (300g) whole-wheat flour*
2 teaspoons sea salt flakes
¼ teaspoon dry yeast powder
1 cup (250ml) water
¼ cup (60ml) olive oil
1 cup (200g) ricotta
2 tablespoons milk
sea salt and cracked black pepper

Place the flour, salt, yeast, water and oil in the bowl of an electric
mixer fitted with a dough hook. Mix for 4 minutes on low speed or
until a smooth dough forms. Cover the dough and allow to stand in
a warm place for 20 minutes or until slightly risen. Divide the dough
into 4 pieces and roll into a thin round. Combine the ricotta, milk,
salt and pepper. Spread each pizza base with the ricotta mixture
then your choice of topping+. Bake in a 200°C (400°F) oven for
14 minutes until the topping is golden and the base is crisp. Serve
with a mixed green salad, if desired. SERVES 4
+ *See toppings for this recipe on the following pages, 112–113.*

POLENTA CRUST TOMATO TART

4 Roma tomatoes, halved
8 sprigs thyme
cracked black pepper
polenta crust
½ cup (75g) plain (all-purpose) flour
1 cup (170g) instant polenta* or cornmeal
120g unsalted butter
⅓ cup (80ml) water
sea salt
filling
300g reduced-fat cream cheese
3 eggs
½ cup chopped basil leaves
⅓ cup (25g) finely grated parmesan

Preheat oven to 200°C (400°F). Place the tomato, cut-side up,
on a baking tray lined with non-stick baking paper. Top with a sprig
of thyme and sprinkle with pepper. Roast for 30 minutes or until
soft. Remove from the oven and set aside.

Reduce heat to 180°C (350°F). To make the polenta crust,
place the flour, polenta, butter, water and salt in a food processor
and process until a dough forms. Press the dough into a 24cm
loose-bottomed tart tin. Top the dough with non-stick baking paper
and fill with baking weights or dried beans. Bake for 15 minutes,
remove the paper and weights or beans and bake for a further
10 minutes or until crisp.

To make the filling, place the cream cheese and egg in a food
processor and process until smooth. Stir through the basil and
parmesan. Pour into the pastry shell and top with the roasted
tomato. Bake for 25 minutes or until the filling has set. Serve
warm with salad greens, if desired. SERVES 4

POLENTA CRUST TOMATO TART

WHOLE-WHEAT PIZZAS – *see page 110 for basic pizza base recipe*

FRESH TOMATO
Top the base with oregano leaves before baking. Top the cooked base with halved mixed cherry tomatoes and finely grated parmesan to serve.

SPINACH *and* FETA
Top the base with blanched baby spinach leaves, crumbled feta, extra ricotta and pine nuts. Serve with a squeeze of lemon.

MUSHROOM
Top the base with sliced mushrooms and thyme leaves. Bake and sprinkle with grated parmesan to serve.

PROSCIUTTO
Top the base with extra spoonfuls of ricotta and sage leaves. Bake and top with prosciutto slices and grated parmesan to serve.

ZUCCHINI *and* MINT
Top the base with thinly sliced zucchini (courgette), salt and pepper. Bake and top with mint and basil leaves to serve.

CARAMELISED ONION
Top the base with store-bought caramelised onion relish*, rosemary leaves, slices of feta and anchovies, if desired.

CRISPY LEMON FISH *with* YOGHURT TARTARE

SOY CHICKEN NOODLE SOUP

CRISPY LEMON FISH *with* YOGHURT TARTARE

1¼ cups (110g) fresh coarse breadcrumbs
2 teaspoons finely grated lemon rind
¼ cup chopped flat-leaf parsley leaves
sea salt and cracked black pepper
8 x 120g firm white fish fillets, skin off
2 tablespoons lemon juice
1 tablespoon olive oil
crispy potato fries, to serve (see *snacks and sides*, page 122)
lemon cheeks, to serve
yoghurt tartare
¾ cup (210g) thick plain yoghurt
2 tablespoons chopped cornichons*
1 tablespoon salted capers, rinsed and chopped
1 tablespoon chopped dill
2 teaspoons white balsamic vinegar

To make the yoghurt tartare, place the yoghurt, cornichons, capers, dill and vinegar in a bowl and mix to combine. Set aside.

Place the breadcrumbs, lemon rind, parsley, salt and pepper in a bowl and mix to combine. Place the fish on a metal baking tray lined with non-stick baking paper and top with the breadcrumb mixture. Combine the lemon juice and oil and drizzle over the breadcrumbs. Cook the fish under a preheated hot grill (broiler) for 5–7 minutes or until the breadcrumbs are crisp and the fish is cooked through. Serve with the yoghurt tartare, crispy potato fries and lemon cheeks. SERVES 4

SOY CHICKEN NOODLE SOUP

2 tablespoons reduced-salt soy sauce
1.5 litres chicken stock
½ cup (125ml) Chinese cooking wine* (Shaoxing)
2 whole star anise
2 cloves garlic, thinly sliced
2 tablespoons brown sugar
2 x 180g chicken breast fillets, trimmed and thickly sliced
200g bok choy, sliced
400g fresh udon noodles*, rinsed
4 spring onions, trimmed and sliced
1 tablespoon finely grated ginger

Place the soy, stock, wine, star anise, garlic and sugar in a saucepan and bring to the boil. Reduce heat to low, add the chicken and simmer for 5 minutes or until the chicken is cooked through. Add the bok choy and noodles and cook for 3 minutes or until tender. Divide the soup between bowls and top with spring onion and ginger to serve. SERVES 4

PEPPERED BEEF *with* FARRO *and* ROASTED VEGETABLES

1 x 750g beef eye fillet, trimmed
vegetable oil, for brushing
1 tablespoon cracked black pepper
sea salt
1½ cups (300g) farro*, well rinsed
3 cups (750ml) chicken stock
1 bunch baby carrots, trimmed and scrubbed
4 eschalots (French shallots), quartered
3 parsnips, peeled, cored and quartered
2 medium-sized field mushrooms, sliced
6 sprigs thyme
1 teaspoon fennel seeds
1 tablespoon olive oil
1 quantity horseradish yoghurt cream (see *basics*, page 182) and freshly grated horseradish* (optional), to serve

Preheat oven to 200°C (400°F). Brush the beef with oil and sprinkle with pepper and salt to coat. Heat a frying pan over high heat. Add the beef and cook for 3–4 minutes each side or until browned. Set aside. Wipe out the pan with absorbent paper. Add the farro and stock and bring to the boil. Reduce heat and simmer for 20 minutes or until farro is tender.

Place the carrot, eschalot, parsnip, mushroom, thyme and fennel in a baking dish, drizzle with oil and toss to coat. Roast for 15 minutes, add the beef to the dish and roast for a further 20 minutes or until the beef is cooked to your liking and the vegetables are tender. Slice the beef and divide between serving plates with the farro and roasted vegetables. Serve with the horseradish cream and freshly grated horseradish. SERVES 4

PEPPERED BEEF *with* FARRO *and* ROASTED VEGETABLES

BABA GHANOUSH

CRISPY POTATO FRIES

BABA GHANOUSH

1 medium eggplant (aubergine)
1 small clove garlic, crushed
¼ cup (70g) thick plain yoghurt
1 tablespoon lemon juice
2 teaspoons tahini paste*
sea salt and cracked black pepper

Place the eggplant on a baking tray lined with non-stick baking
paper and place under a preheated hoy grill (broiler). Cook for
10 minutes each side or until the skin is toasted and black and the
flesh is soft. Allow to cool slightly before peeling and discarding the
skin. Place the eggplant flesh, garlic, yoghurt, lemon juice, tahini,
salt and pepper in a food processor and process until smooth.
Serve with vegetable sticks or as a condiment. SERVES 4

CRISPY POTATO FRIES

3 large starchy potatoes, scrubbed
2 tablespoons vegetable oil
2 tablespoons rosemary leaves
sea salt

Preheat oven to 200°C (400°F). Cut the potatoes into thin fries.
Place on absorbent paper and pat dry. Place in a large bowl with
the oil, rosemary and salt and toss well to coat. Divide the potatoes
in a single layer between two baking trays lined with non-stick
baking paper and bake for 20 minutes. Turn the fries and bake for
a further 10 minutes or until the fries are crisp and golden. SERVES 4

SPICED CHICKPEAS

1 x 400g can chickpeas (garbanzos), drained and rinsed
2 teaspoons vegetable oil
¼ teaspoon fennel seeds
¼ teaspoon cayenne pepper
2 teaspoons finely grated lemon rind
½ teaspoon table salt
1 teaspoon caster sugar

Place the chickpeas on absorbent paper and pat dry. Heat the oil
in a non-stick frying pan over high heat. Add the fennel, cayenne,
lemon, salt and sugar and cook, stirring, for 1 minute until fragrant.
Add the chickpeas and cook, stirring, for 7–10 minutes or until
slightly crisp. Serve warm or cold. SERVES 4

These chickpeas are my ADDICTIVE *new party snack. They've got robust hints of
spice and lemon and are* BETTER *than indulging in greasy snacks. I've also included
a* VIRTUOUS *oven-baked fry, so you don't need to skip the chips every time!*

SPICED CHICKPEAS

Flavoured HUMMUS *makes a great* SNACK OR CONDIMENT

HUMMUS

ROASTED CARROT *and* FENNEL
Place ¾ cup drained canned chickpeas (garbanzos), 1 cup chopped roasted carrot, ½ teaspoon toasted fennel seeds, ¼ cup (60ml) tahini paste*, 1 teaspoon grated ginger, ¼ cup (60ml) each water and orange juice, ½ cup coriander (cilantro) leaves and salt in a food processor and process until smooth. SERVES 4

GREEN PEA *and* CORIANDER
Place 1 cup (120g) blanched peas, ¼ cup chopped coriander (cilantro) leaves, 2 tablespoons each tahini paste* and lemon juice, 1 tablespoon water, ½ clove crushed garlic, salt and pepper in a food processor and pulse until roughly chopped. Serve with flatbread or vegetables. SERVES 4

HUMMUS
Place 1 x 400g can drained chickpeas (garbanzos), 2 tablespoons tahini paste*, ½ clove crushed garlic, 2 tablespoons each thick plain yoghurt and lemon juice, ¼ cup (60ml) water, salt and pepper in a food processor and process until smooth. Serve as a dip or condiment. SERVES 4

LEMON, SESAME and CHILLI

Place 1 x 400g can drained chickpeas (garbanzos), ⅓ cup (80ml) water, 1 clove crushed garlic, 1 tablespoon each lemon juice and finely grated lemon rind in a food processor and process until smooth. Stir through 3 tablespoons sesame seeds, 1 long seeded and chopped red chilli and salt to serve. SERVES 4

LENTIL and PARSLEY

Place 1 x 400g can drained and rinsed brown lentils, 2 tablespoons each crunchy peanut butter and lemon juice, 1 tablespoon water, 1 long seeded and chopped red chilli, 1 cup flat-leaf parsley leaves, salt and pepper in a food processor and pulse until a rough paste forms. SERVES 4

EDAMAME and WASABI

Place 1 cup (120g) blanched edamame (baby soy beans), ⅓ cup silken tofu*, 1 teaspoon wasabi paste*, 1 teaspoon soy sauce and sea salt in a food processor and process until smooth. Serve with flatbread or vegetables. SERVES 4

SPICY SWEET POTATO WEDGES

SPICY SWEET POTATO WEDGES

1kg sweet potato (kumara), peeled and cut into thin wedges
2 teaspoons olive oil
1 teaspoon dried chilli flakes
½ teaspoon sumac*
½ teaspoon sea salt flakes

Preheat oven to 200°C (400°F). Place the sweet potato in a bowl, add the oil and toss to coat. Add the chilli, sumac and salt and toss to coat. Place the potato in a single layer on 2 baking trays lined with non-stick baking paper and bake for 15 minutes, turn and bake for a further 10 minutes or until crisp. SERVES 4

KALE CHIPS

200g kale leaves, trimmed and cut into large chunks
1½ tablespoons vegetable oil
½ teaspoon sea salt flakes
½ teaspoon Chinese five-spice powder*
½ teaspoon dried chilli flakes

Preheat oven to 180°C (350°F). Place the kale in a large bowl with the oil and toss to coat. Combine the salt, five spice and chilli, sprinkle over the kale and toss to coat. Place the kale on 2 baking trays lined with non-stick baking paper and bake for 8–10 minutes or until crisp. SERVES 4

Who would have thought that two of the HEALTHIEST *vegetables in your crisper could be* SPICED *up to become a crisp, glam snack. Beautiful emerald green kale crunches up to perfection, while sweet potato gets a spicy* IRRESISTIBLE *coating.*

KALE CHIPS

FETA, OLIVE *and* YOGHURT DIP

FETA, OLIVE *and* YOGHURT DIP

100g feta
½ cup (140g) thick plain yoghurt
1 tablespoon lemon juice
1 tablespoon oregano leaves
20 green olives, pitted
cracked black pepper

Place the feta, yoghurt and lemon in a blender or food processor
and process until smooth. Add the oregano, olives and pepper and
blend until finely chopped. Serve with cucumber and celery sticks.
SERVES 4

BRUSSELS SPROUTS *and* RICOTTA GRATIN

1½ cups (300g) ricotta
⅔ cup (50g) finely grated parmesan
2 eggs
1½ cups (375ml) milk
sea salt and cracked black pepper
18 Brussels sprouts, trimmed and halved
2 teaspoons lemon thyme leaves

Preheat oven to 180°C (350°F). Place the ricotta, parmesan, egg,
milk, salt and pepper in a bowl and whisk to combine. Pour the
mixture into the base of a 2 litre-capacity ovenproof dish. Arrange
the sprouts, cut-side up, on top of the ricotta mixture and sprinkle
with the thyme. Bake for 45 minutes or until the sprouts are tender.
SERVES 4

If you have nothing but MEMORIES *of eating bland boiled sprouts as a child, here's
a recipe that will sway you to learn to love the sprout! Baked to a* GOLDEN *glow and
partnered with* CREAMY *lemon-spiked ricotta, it makes for a delicious side dish.*

BRUSSELS SPROUTS *and* RICOTTA GRATIN

SPICED QUINOA PILAF

SHAVED ASPARAGUS SALAD

SPICED QUINOA PILAF

1 teaspoon vegetable oil
1 teaspoon ground cumin
½ teaspoon dried chilli flakes
2 cloves garlic, sliced
1 cup (200g) white quinoa*
1½ cups (375ml) chicken or vegetable stock
coriander (cilantro) leaves, to serve

Heat a saucepan over medium–high heat. Add the oil, cumin and
chilli and cook for 1–2 minutes or until fragrant. Add the garlic and
cook, stirring, for 30 seconds. Add the quinoa and stock and bring
to the boil. Reduce heat to low and cover with a tight-fitting lid.
Cook for 12–14 minutes or until quinoa is tender and the stock is
absorbed. Top with the coriander leaves and serve with roasted lamb
or grilled meats. SERVES 4

SHAVED ASPARAGUS SALAD

2 cups (240g) chunky sourdough breadcrumbs
3 cloves garlic, sliced
2 tablespoons salted capers, rinsed
1 tablespoon olive oil
10 stalks green asparagus
10 stalks white asparagus
½ cup chervil sprigs
1 quantity lemon buttermilk dressing (see *basics*, page 185)

Preheat oven to 180°C (350°F). Place the breadcrumbs, garlic
and capers on a baking tray lined with non-stick baking paper and
sprinkle with the oil. Bake for 10 minutes or until the crumbs and
garlic are golden. Set aside.

Trim the asparagus and shave thinly with a vegetable peeler.
Combine the asparagus with the crumb mixture, divide between
serving plates and top with the chervil. Serve with the lemon
buttermilk dressing. SERVES 4-6

BALSAMIC-GLAZED BEETROOT

2 bunches baby beetroot, trimmed
1 cup (250ml) balsamic vinegar
½ cup (90g) brown sugar
4 sprigs thyme

Place the beetroot in a saucepan of boiling water and cook for
8–10 minutes or until tender. Drain and peel away the skins.
Place the balsamic, sugar and thyme in a frying pan over medium
heat and simmer for 5 minutes or until thickened. Add the beets
and toss to coat. SERVES 4

These sweet glazed baby beetroot are really VERSATILE *and are at home in many
dishes. They're equally good in a salad or served with* ROASTED *or grilled meats
or sliced and layered in a beef or lamb* BURGER *in true Australian fashion!*

BALSAMIC-GLAZED BEETROOT

EDAMAME

GARLIC
Cook 400g thawed edamame (baby soy beans) in a large saucepan of generously salted water over high heat for 2–3 minutes or until tender and drain. Fry 2 cloves thinly sliced garlic in 2 teaspoons vegetable oil until light golden. Add the cooked edamame and sea salt and toss to combine.

SESAME SALT
Cook 400g thawed edamame (baby soy beans) in a large saucepan of generously salted water over high heat for 2–3 minutes or until tender and drain. Place 1 tablespoon toasted sesame seeds and 1 teaspoon sea salt flakes in a mortar and pestle and grind until well combined. Toss through the cooked edamame beans to serve.

SOY *and* LEMON
Cook 400g thawed edamame (baby soy beans) in a large saucepan of generously salted water over high heat for 2–3 minutes or until tender and drain. Combine the cooked edamame with 2 tablespoons lemon juice and 1 tablespoon soy sauce to serve.

These little FRESH SNACKS *are packed with* FLAVOUR

LEMON *and* PEPPER

Cook 400g thawed edamame (baby soy beans) in a large saucepan of generously salted water over high heat for 2–3 minutes or until tender and drain. Combine the cooked edamame, 2 teaspoons sea salt flakes, 1 teaspoon finely grated lemon rind and ½ teaspoon cracked black pepper to serve.

CRISPY GINGER

Cook 400g thawed edamame (baby soy beans) in a large saucepan of generously salted water over high heat for 2–3 minutes or until tender and drain. Fry 1 tablespoon shredded ginger in 2 teaspoons vegetable oil until crisp. Add the cooked edamame and sea salt and toss to combine.

CHILLI SALT

Cook 400g thawed edamame (baby soy beans) in a large saucepan of generously salted water over high heat for 2–3 minutes or until tender and drain. Place 2 teaspoons dried chilli flakes and 1 tablespoon sea salt flakes in a mortar and pestle and grind to combine. Toss through the cooked edamame to serve.

KALE SLAW

KALE SLAW

5 stalks kale, stems removed and shredded
1 bulb fennel, finely sliced using a mandolin
5 stalks silver beet, stems removed and shredded
50g baby rocket (arugula) leaves
½ cup (80g) pine nuts or slivered almonds, toasted
½ cup flat-leaf parsley leaves
¼ cup snipped chives
1 quantity lemon buttermilk dressing (see *basics*, page 185)

Place the kale, fennel, silver beet, rocket, pine nuts, parsley and chives in a bowl and toss gently to combine. Pour over the dressing and toss gently to coat. SERVES 4

CELERIAC *and* PARSNIP PURÉE

700g celeriac (celery root), peeled and chopped
2 parsnips, peeled, cored and chopped
4 sprigs thyme
1 cup (250ml) vegetable or chicken stock
150g ricotta
sea salt flakes

Place the celeriac, parsnip, thyme and stock in a deep frying pan and bring to the boil. Cover and cook for 10 minutes or until the vegetables are soft. Remove the thyme and set aside. Place the vegetables in a food processor and process until smooth. Add the ricotta and salt and process until smooth. Return the mixture to the saucepan and stir over low heat until warmed through. Top with the thyme and serve with roasted or grilled meats. SERVES 4

This power slaw has all the makings of a PERFECT *salad. It's got a crunchy bite and creamy* TEXTURE *and is packed with fresh herbs and plenty of goodness. It's my new favourite go-to salad for a* QUICK *weeknight meal or a weekend barbecue spread.*

CELERIAC *and* PARSNIP PURÉE

MISO *and* SESAME BROCCOLI

MISO *and* SESAME BROCCOLI

1 tablespoon sesame seeds
1 tablespoon yellow miso paste*
2 tablespoons mirin*
¼ cup (60ml) chicken or vegetable stock
1 teaspoon finely grated ginger
500g broccoli, cut into florets

Heat a deep non-stick frying pan over medium heat. Add the
sesame seeds and cook, stirring, for 3 minutes or until toasted.
Add the miso, mirin, stock and ginger and cook for 2 minutes.
Add the broccoli and toss to coat. Cover and cook for 3–4 minutes
or until the broccoli is just tender. Serve with poached or grilled
chicken. SERVES 4

GINGER *and* SOY CABBAGE

1 tablespoon vegetable oil
2 tablespoons shredded ginger
2 long red chillies, seeds removed and sliced
4 cloves garlic, sliced
500g white cabbage, cut into wedges
2 tablespoons Chinese rice wine* (Shaoxing)
2 tablespoons soy sauce
toasted sesame seeds, to serve

Heat the oil in a large non-stick frying pan or wok over high heat.
Add the ginger, chilli and garlic and cook, stirring, for 1 minute. Add
the cabbage and cook, stirring, for 2 minutes. Add the wine and soy
and cook for a further 2 minutes or until the cabbage is just tender.
Sprinkle with the sesame seeds to serve. SERVES 4

Big POWERFUL *greens like broccoli and cabbage demand some equally gutsy flavours
alongside them. This cabbage dish is paired with* ROBUST *garlic, ginger and chilli, while
salty-sweet* MISO *makes a great partner for broccoli. Try them with poached chicken.*

GINGER *and* SOY CABBAGE

DESSERTS *and* TREATS

I'm all for SPLURGING on dessert and will tend to find room for something
SWEET at the end of a meal. But that doesn't mean it always has to be naughty.
These are my ideas for a sweet finale or a little treat with a LIGHTER touch.
So you can still INDULGE in the flavours you love but feel a little more innocent
doing it! From creamy bites to fruity delights, it's time to TREAT yourself.

CHOCOLATE CHIP COOKIES

CHOCOLATE FUDGE CAKE

CHOCOLATE CHIP COOKIES

2 cups (300g) plain (all-purpose) wholemeal flour
½ cup (45g) rolled oats
½ teaspoon baking powder
½ cup (110g) caster (superfine) sugar
120g dark chocolate, coarsely chopped
½ cup (125ml) vegetable oil
½ cup (125ml) maple syrup
1 egg
1½ teaspoons vanilla extract

Preheat oven to 180°C (350°F). Place the flour, oats, baking powder, sugar and chocolate in a bowl and mix to combine. Make a well in the centre and add the oil, maple syrup, egg and vanilla and mix to combine. Roll heaped tablespoonfuls of the mixture into balls and place on baking trays lined with non-stick baking paper, allowing room to spread. Flatten the cookies slightly and bake for 12–15 minutes or until golden. Cool on trays. MAKES 18

CHOCOLATE FUDGE CAKE

¾ cup (115g) plain (all-purpose) flour, sifted
½ teaspoon baking powder
¾ cup (75g) cocoa, sifted
1½ cups (265g) brown sugar
3 eggs
¾ cup (180ml) buttermilk
1 teaspoon vanilla extract
⅓ cup (80ml) vegetable oil
cocoa, extra, for dusting

Preheat oven to 160°C (325°F). Place the flour, baking powder, cocoa and sugar in a bowl and mix to combine. In a separate bowl, whisk together the eggs, buttermilk, vanilla and oil. Pour into the dry mixture and mix until smooth. Pour the cake mixture into a 20cm square cake tin lined with non-stick baking paper. Bake for 40 minutes or until just firm. Cool in the tin, dust with cocoa and cut into squares to serve. MAKES 25 SQUARES

CHOCOLATE, PISTACHIO *and* ALMOND BISCOTTI

2 cups (300g) plain (all-purpose) whole-wheat flour*, sifted
⅓ cup (35g) cocoa, sifted
2 teaspoons baking powder
1 cup (175g) brown sugar
½ cup (80g) blanched almonds
⅓ cup (45g) unsalted shelled pistachios
2 eggs, lightly beaten
¼ cup (60ml) milk

Preheat oven to 160°C (325°F). Place the flour, cocoa and baking powder in a bowl. Add the sugar, almonds and pistachios and mix well. Add the eggs and milk and mix until a firm dough forms. (This may take some time.)

Knead the dough on a lightly floured surface until smooth. Divide mixture in half and shape into 2 logs. Place on baking trays lined with non-stick baking paper and bake for 35–40 minutes or until firm. Allow to cool.

Reduce heat to 140°C (275°F). Using a serrated knife, cut each log into thin slices and place on baking trays lined with non-stick baking paper. Bake for 15–20 minutes or until crisp. Store in an airtight container for up to 1 week. MAKES 50

CHOCOLATE, PISTACHIO *and* ALMOND BISCOTTI

GRANITA

COCONUT *and* LIME
Mix to combine 1 cup (250ml) water, 1½ cups (375ml) coconut milk⁺, 2 tablespoons lime juice and ⅓ cup (75g) caster (superfine) sugar. Pour the mixture into a shallow metal tin and freeze until firm. Rake the top of the granita with a fork to serve.

BLOOD ORANGE
Mix to combine 2 cups (500ml) blood orange juice and ¼ cup (60ml) light agave syrup (nectar)*. Pour the mixture into a shallow metal tin and freeze until firm. Rake the top of the granita with a fork to serve.

WATERMELON
Mix to combine 2 cups (500ml) fresh watermelon juice and ¼ cup (60ml) light agave syrup (nectar)*. Pour the mixture into a shallow metal tin and freeze until firm. Rake the top of the granita with a fork to serve.

Cool TREATS *full of fruity* FLAVOUR

LATTE
Mix to combine 2 cups (500ml) milk,
⅓ cup (80ml) strong cooled espresso and
¼ cup (60ml) light agave syrup (nectar)*.
Pour the mixture into a shallow metal tin
and freeze until firm. Rake the top of the
granita with a fork to serve.

HONEYDEW MELON
Mix to combine 2 cups (500ml) fresh
honeydew melon juice and ¼ cup (60ml)
light agave syrup (nectar)*. Pour the mixture
into a shallow metal tin and freeze until
firm. Rake the top of the granita with a
fork to serve.

RASPBERRY
Blend 2 cups (300g) thawed frozen
raspberries with 2 cups (500ml) water.
Strain and combine with ¼ cup (60ml)
light agave syrup (nectar)*. Pour the mixture
into a shallow metal tin and freeze until
firm. Rake the top of the granita with a
fork to serve.

PEAR TART

PEAR TART

¾ cup (115g) plain (all-purpose) whole-wheat flour*
⅓ cup (40g) almond meal (ground almonds)
1½ teaspoons baking powder
⅓ cup (80ml) maple syrup or light agave syrup (nectar)*
1 egg
¾ cup (180ml) buttermilk
2 teaspoons finely grated lemon rind
½ teaspoon ground cinnamon
40g unsalted butter, melted
2 firm brown pears, peeled, cored and sliced
2 tablespoons raw sugar
1 quantity whipped vanilla ricotta (see *basics*, page 176), to serve

Preheat oven to 190°C (375°F). Place the flour, almond meal and baking powder in a bowl and mix to combine. In a separate bowl, mix together the maple syrup, egg, buttermilk, lemon rind and cinnamon. Add the buttermilk mixture to the dry ingredients with the butter and mix to combine. Line the base of a greased 24cm loose-bottomed tart tin with non-stick baking paper. Pour the mixture into the tin and smooth the top. Arrange the pears over the top and sprinkle with sugar. Bake for 35–40 minutes or until the tart is cooked when tested with a skewer. Serve warm with the whipped vanilla ricotta. SERVES 8-10

APPLE TARTS

30g unsalted butter
2 tablespoons maple syrup
½ teaspoon ground cinnamon
6 sheets filo (phyllo) pastry
1 red apple, very thinly sliced using a mandolin
white sugar, for sprinkling
1 quantity whipped vanilla ricotta (see *basics*, page 176), to serve

Preheat oven to 180°C (350°F). Place the butter, maple syrup and cinnamon in a saucepan over low heat and cook until the butter has melted. Lightly brush a sheet of the pastry with the butter mixture and top with another sheet of pastry. Repeat until all the pastry has been used. Cut the pastry stack into 6 rectangles. Place the stacks on a baking tray lined with non-stick baking paper. Top the pastry with the apple and sprinkle with a little sugar. Bake for 10 minutes or until golden and crisp. Serve warm with the whipped vanilla ricotta. SERVES 6

I've started baking a few sweets with WHOLE-WHEAT *flour and it has such a lovely nutty, well-rounded* TASTE. *The flour has body and flavour, much like a really good sourdough bread. The addition of almond meal to this tart keeps it beautifully* MOIST.

APPLE TARTS

LEMON *and* YOGHURT PANNA COTTA

LEMON *and* YOGHURT PANNA COTTA

1 tablespoon cold water
¾ teaspoon powdered gelatine*
1 cup (250ml) milk
¼ cup (55g) caster (superfine) sugar
2 teaspoons finely grated lemon rind
1¼ cups (350g) vanilla yoghurt

Place the water in a small bowl and sprinkle over the gelatine.
Allow to stand for 5 minutes or the water has been absorbed.
Place the milk and sugar in a saucepan over medium heat
and heat until hot, but not boiling. Add the gelatine and stir
continuously for 1 minute. Remove from the heat and allow to
cool slightly. Whisk in the lemon rind and yoghurt and pour into
4 serving glasses or bowls. Refrigerate for 4 hours or until set.
Serve with fresh berries, if desired. SERVES 4

BERRY *and* RICOTTA SLICE

400g ricotta
125g reduced-fat cream cheese
2 eggs
¼ cup (60ml) lemon juice
2 teaspoons vanilla extract
1 tablespoon rice flour*
½ cup (110g) caster (superfine) sugar
fresh berries, to serve

Preheat oven to 160°C (325°F). Place the ricotta, cream cheese,
egg, lemon juice, vanilla, rice flour and sugar in a food processor and
process until smooth. Spoon the mixture into a 20cm x 30cm slice
tin lined with non-stick baking paper. Bake for 20 minutes or until
firm. Refrigerate until cold. Top with fresh berries to serve. SERVES 12

BASIC BANANA BREAD

1 cup (150g) self-raising (self-rising) flour, sifted
1 cup (150g) self-raising (self-rising) whole-wheat flour*, sifted
2 teaspoons baking powder
¾ cup (135g) brown sugar
½ teaspoon ground cinnamon
1½ cups (375g) mashed banana
⅓ cup (80ml) vegetable oil
¾ cup (180ml) buttermilk
2 eggs
1 teaspoon vanilla extract

Preheat oven to 180°C (350°F). Place the flours, baking powder,
sugar and cinnamon in a bowl and mix to combine. Add the banana,
oil, buttermilk, egg and vanilla and mix until smooth. If using, stir
through the fruit and other ingredients[+]. Spoon the mixture into a
greased 11cm x 26cm loaf tin lined with non-stick baking paper.
Bake for 40–45 minutes or until cooked when tested with
a skewer. Serve warm or cold. SERVES 10
+ *See fillings and variations for this recipe on the following pages,
158–159. You can freeze this banana bread for up to 1 month.*

BERRY *and* RICOTTA SLICE

BANANA BREAD – *see page 156 for basic recipe*

BLUEBERRY
Mix 1 cup (150g) fresh or frozen blueberries through the basic mixture and then add 5 minutes to the cooking time.
+ *If using frozen berries, do not thaw the berries first.*

MAPLE SYRUP
Add ¼ cup (60ml) maple syrup to the basic mixture with the wet ingredients.

MANGO COCONUT
Mix ¾ cup (150g) chopped mango and ¼ cup (20g) shredded coconut through the basic mixture and then add 5 minutes to the cooking time.

Delicious BANANA BREAD *makes a* SWEET SNACK

CRANBERRY
Mix 1 cup (130g) sweetened dried cranberries through the basic mixture.

DATE
Mix 1 cup (140g) pitted and chopped fresh dates through the basic mixture.

RASPBERRY
Mix 1 cup (150g) fresh or frozen raspberries through the basic mixture and then add 5 minutes to the original cooking time.
+ *If using frozen berries, do not thaw the berries first.*

BAKED RICOTTA CHEESECAKE

CARROT CAKE *with* CREAM CHEESE FROSTING

BAKED RICOTTA CHEESECAKE

650g ricotta
250g reduced-fat cream cheese
1 cup (280g) reduced-fat plain yoghurt
1 tablespoon cornflour (cornstarch)
⅓ cup (80ml) lemon juice
1 tablespoon finely grated lemon rind
1 teaspoon vanilla extract
3 eggs
1 cup (220g) caster (superfine) sugar

Preheat oven to 160°C (325°F). Place the ricotta, cream cheese and yoghurt in a food processor and process until smooth. Place the cornflour in a small bowl, add the lemon juice and mix until smooth. Add to the cheese mixture with the lemon rind, vanilla, eggs and sugar. Process until smooth. Pour the mixture into a greased 20cm springform tin lined with non-stick baking paper. Bake for 50–55 minutes or until just set and slightly golden. Refrigerate in the tin until chilled. SERVES 12

CARROT CAKE *with* CREAM CHEESE FROSTING

1 cup (150g) self-raising (self-rising) flour, sifted
1 cup (150g) self-raising (self-rising) whole-wheat flour*
1 teaspoon baking powder
¾ cup (135g) brown sugar
¼ cup (55g) caster (superfine) sugar
1 teaspoon ground cinnamon
3 eggs
¼ cup (60ml) vegetable oil
1½ cups (360g) grated carrot (approximately 3 carrots)
1 cup (180g) grated zucchini (courgette) (approximately
    2 small zucchini)
cream cheese frosting
150g reduced-fat cream cheese
¼ cup (60ml) light agave syrup (nectar)*
2 teaspoons finely grated lemon rind

Preheat oven to 180°C (350°F). Place the flours, baking powder, sugars and cinnamon in a bowl and mix to combine. In a separate bowl, mix together the eggs and oil and add to the dry ingredients with the carrot and zucchini. Mix until combined. Pour the mixture into a greased 20cm round cake tin lined with non-stick baking paper. Bake for 45–50 minutes or until cooked when tested with a skewer. Cool in the tin for 5 minutes, turn out onto a wire rack and cool.

To make the frosting, place the cream cheese, agave syrup, and lemon in a food processor and process until smooth. Using a palette knife, spread the icing over the cooled cake to serve. SERVES 12

RASPBERRY FROZEN YOGHURT

125g frozen raspberries
2 cups (560g) thick plain yoghurt
¼ cup (60ml) light agave syrup (nectar)* or maple syrup
1 teaspoon vanilla extract

Place the berries, yoghurt, agave syrup and vanilla in an ice-cream machine and churn for 25 minutes or until thick enough to scoop. Freeze until firm. SERVES 6–8
+ *For other flavour variations, see the recipes below.*

PASSIONFRUIT FROZEN YOGHURT

½ cup (125ml) passionfruit pulp (approximately 4 passionfruit)
2 cups (560g) thick plain yoghurt
¼ cup (60ml) light agave syrup (nectar)* or maple syrup
1 teaspoon vanilla extract

Place the passionfruit pulp, yoghurt, agave syrup and vanilla in an ice-cream machine and churn for 25 minutes or until thick enough to scoop. Freeze until firm. SERVES 6–8

MANGO FROZEN YOGHURT

¾ cup (150g) mango, peeled and finely chopped
2 cups (560g) thick plain yoghurt
¼ cup (60ml) light agave syrup (nectar)* or maple syrup
1 teaspoon vanilla extract

Place the mango, yoghurt, agave syrup and vanilla in an ice-cream machine and churn for 25 minutes or until thick enough to scoop. Freeze until firm. SERVES 6–8

RASPBERRY FROZEN YOGHURT

POPSICLES

HONEY
Place 1½ cups (420g) reduced-fat vanilla yoghurt, ½ cup (125ml) milk and ¼ cup (90g) honey in a bowl and mix to combine. Pour into popsicle moulds and freeze until solid.

RASPBERRY
Place 1½ cups (420g) reduced-fat vanilla yoghurt, ½ cup (125ml) milk and ¼ cup (60ml) light agave syrup (nectar)* in a bowl and mix to combine. Stir in ¾ cup (120g) fresh or frozen raspberries. Pour into popsicle moulds and freeze until solid.

BANANA MAPLE
Place 1 cup (280g) reduced-fat vanilla yoghurt, ½ cup (125ml) milk, ¼ cup (60ml) maple syrup and 1 banana in a blender and blend until smooth. Pour into popsicle moulds and freeze until solid.

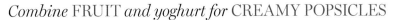

Combine FRUIT *and yoghurt for* CREAMY POPSICLES

MANGO
Place 1½ cups (420g) reduced-fat vanilla yoghurt, ½ cup (125ml) milk, 2 mango cheeks and ¼ cup (60ml) light agave syrup (nectar)* in a blender and blend until smooth. Pour into popsicle moulds and freeze until solid.

BANANA BERRY
Place 1 cup (280g) reduced-fat vanilla yoghurt, ½ cup (125ml) milk, 1 banana, 1 cup (150g) fresh or frozen blueberries and ¼ cup (90g) honey in a blender and blend until smooth. Pour into popsicle moulds and freeze until solid.

STRAWBERRY
Place 2 cups (560g) reduced-fat vanilla yoghurt and ½ cup (160g) sugar-free strawberry jam in a bowl and whisk to combine. Stir through ½ cup (65g) finely sliced strawberries and pour into popsicle moulds. Freeze until solid.

BAKED FIGS *in* BUTTERMILK CUSTARD

MANGO *and* ALMOND PIES

MANGO *and* ALMOND PIES

60g unsalted butter, softened
1½ cups (180g) almond meal (ground almonds)
1 tablespoon finely grated lemon rind
1 cup (150g) self-raising (self-rising) flour, sifted
4 eggs
¾ cup (165g) caster (superfine) sugar
2 mangoes, peeled and cut into thick wedges
white sugar, for sprinkling
1 quantity whipped vanilla ricotta (see *basics*, page 176), to serve

Preheat oven to 160°C (325°F). Place the butter, almond meal, lemon rind, flour, eggs and sugar in a bowl and mix to combine. Spoon the mixture into 4 lightly greased pie dishes or small ovenproof dishes. Top with the mango and sprinkle with a little sugar. Bake for 30–35 minutes or until golden. Serve warm with the whipped vanilla ricotta. SERVES 4

MIXED BERRY COBBLER

750g frozen mixed berries
3 apples, peeled, cored and chopped
1½ tablespoons cornflour (cornstarch)
⅓ cup (75g) caster (superfine) sugar
golden buttermilk topping
½ cup (75g) self-raising (self-rising) whole-wheat flour*
½ cup (75g) self-raising (self-rising) flour
1 teaspoon baking powder
⅓ cup (30g) rolled oats
1 teaspoon ground cinnamon
¼ cup (30g) almond meal (ground almonds)
½ cup (110g) raw sugar
60g unsalted butter, chopped
1 cup (250ml) buttermilk
extra raw sugar, for sprinkling

Preheat oven to 180°C (350°F). Place the berries, apple, cornflour and sugar in a bowl and toss to combine. Place in a 2.5 litre-capacity ovenproof dish.

To make the golden buttermilk topping, place the flours, baking powder, oats, cinnamon, almond meal and sugar in a bowl. Add the butter and rub with your fingertips to combine. Add the buttermilk and mix until combined. Spoon the cobbler mixture in large spoonfuls over the fruit. Sprinkle with the extra sugar. Bake for 1 hour 20 minutes or until the cobbler is puffed and golden and cooked when tested with a skewer. SERVES 6-8

Here's a spin on a winter pudding that's warming and GENEROUS *but not too rich. Like its cousin the crumble,* COBBLER *has a golden topping rather than a base. I've used whole-wheat flour, almond meal and tangy buttermilk for a* LIGHTER *touch.*

MIXED BERRY COBBLER

BASICS

This chapter is filled with handy ALTERNATIVES or lighter versions of some basic CONDIMENTS and sides that you should have on hand in the kitchen. There are dressings, dips and other ACCOMPANIMENTS that span breakfast to dinner, as well as BASIC cooking methods and techniques for staple ingredients, from chicken to quinoa, that will make it EASIER to use this book.

WHIPPED VANILLA RICOTTA

YOGHURT CHEESE

WHIPPED VANILLA RICOTTA

200g ricotta
2 tablespoons maple syrup
1 teaspoon vanilla extract

Place the ricotta, maple syrup and vanilla in a bowl and whisk to combine. Store in an airtight container in the refrigerator for up to 1 week. MAKES 1 CUP (250G)
+ *This makes a great alternative to double (thick) cream or ice-cream when serving with desserts and cakes. You could also serve it with pancakes or crumpets or even spread it on toasted banana bread.*

YOGHURT CHEESE

1kg thick plain yoghurt
1 teaspoon sea salt flakes

Mix together the yoghurt and salt. Place the mixture in the centre of a piece of clean muslin and gather up the edges to enclose. Tie with string and hang the yoghurt over a bowl in the refrigerator to drain for 8 hours or overnight, until firm. Store in an airtight container in the refrigerator for up to 1 week. You can flavour the cheese by adding finely grated lemon rind, chopped herbs, pepper or dried chilli flakes. MAKES 2⅓ CUPS (580G)
+ *This cheese is also known as labna in the Middle East. You could serve it as you would feta. Try it on a mezze plate, served with flatbread. Alternatively, you could toss it through a salad or use it in a frittata.*

VANILLA YOGHURT

1 cup (280g) thick plain yoghurt
1 teaspoon vanilla extract
2 tablespoons light agave syrup (nectar)* or maple syrup

Place the yoghurt, vanilla and agave syrup in a bowl and whisk to combine. Store in an airtight container in the refrigerator for up to 1 week. MAKES 1 CUP (300G)
+ *Making your own vanilla-flavoured yoghurt allows you to balance the sweetness and vanilla flavour perfectly. Serve this with granola or muesli for breakfast, top with fresh fruit as a quick snack or serve with cakes and desserts as an alternative to cream.*

Don't you wish that sometimes you could serve DESSERT without the heavy cream or ice-cream? This WHIPPED ricotta and vanilla yoghurt make a great alternative to serve with puddings, syrup cakes and other desserts, minus the GUILT, of course!

VANILLA YOGHURT

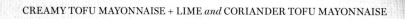

CREAMY TOFU MAYONNAISE + LIME *and* CORIANDER TOFU MAYONNAISE

CREAMY TOFU MAYONNAISE

300g silken tofu*
1 tablepsoon white vinegar
1 teaspoon Dijon mustard
sea salt and cracked black pepper

Place the tofu, vinegar, mustard, salt and pepper in a blender
or food processor and process until smooth. Serve as you would
mayonnaise. Refrigerate for up to 10 days, or for the shelf-life
of the tofu you are using. MAKES 1¼ CUPS (310G)

LIME *and* CORIANDER
TOFU MAYONNAISE

300g silken tofu*
¼ cup (60ml) lime juice
⅓ cup coriander (cilantro) leaves
sea salt and cracked black pepper

Place the tofu, lime, coriander, salt and pepper in a blender or
food processor and process until smooth. Serve as you would
mayonnaise. Refrigerate for up to 10 days, or for the shelf-life
of the tofu you are using. MAKES 1¼ CUPS (375G)

BASIC QUINOA

1½ cups (300g) white quinoa*, rinsed
2 cups (500ml) chicken or vegetable stock

Place the quinoa and stock in a saucepan over medium–high
heat and bring to the boil. Reduce heat to low, cover and cook
for 12–14 minutes or until the stock has been absorbed and the
quinoa is tender. Remove from the heat and stand for 5 minutes.
Stir with a fork to separate the grains and serve hot or cold.
Store cooked quinoa in an airtight container in the refrigerator
for up to 2–3 days. SERVES 4

Don't be put off by the use of silken tofu in this MAYONNAISE – *it actually gives this condiment* SUBSTANCE *and a creamy texture, plus the bonus of extra protein. Use it on sandwiches, in burgers or in a salad dressing. The lime version is especially* TASTY.

BASIC QUINOA

HORSERADISH YOGHURT CREAM

HORSERADISH YOGHURT CREAM

⅓ cup (90g) thick plain yoghurt
1 tablespoon freshly grated horseradish*
1 teaspoon Dijon mustard
sea salt and cracked black pepper

Place the yoghurt, horseradish, mustard, salt and pepper in a bowl and mix to combine. Serve with grilled, barbecued or roasted meats. MAKES ⅓ CUP (90G)
+ *This is particularly good with roasted beef and also makes a great condiment with roasted vegetables, spread on sandwiches or used in a salad dressing. Try it in a potato salad.*

LEMON POACHED CHICKEN

1 litre chicken stock
1 lemon, sliced
4 sprigs lemon thyme
1 teaspoon peppercorns
4 x 180g chicken breast fillets, trimmed

Place the stock, lemon, thyme and peppercorns in a deep frying pan over high heat and bring to the boil. Add the chicken and cook for 3 minutes. Remove from the heat, cover with a lid and stand for 10 minutes or until the chicken is cooked through. SERVES 4
+ *Once you've poached the chicken you can use it in myriad dishes. Shred the meat and use in salads and sandwiches or even in soup. The poached chicken will keep in the refrigerator for up to 2 days.*

POACHED *chicken is incredibly versatile and is one of your best friends in the kitchen. Use it in sandwiches or slice and shred it through* SALADS*, pastas, frittatas or soups. For an* ASIAN *flavour, you could poach the chicken with lemongrass, ginger and chilli.*

LEMON POACHED CHICKEN

Try these VIBRANT *dressings in* FRESH SALADS

DRESSINGS

HUMMUS DRESSING
Place 1 cup (200g) drained canned chickpeas (garbanzos), ¼ cup (60ml) tahini paste*, 2 tablespoons lemon juice, ½ cup (125ml) water, 1 clove crushed garlic, a pinch ground cumin, salt and pepper in a blender or food processor and process until smooth. Refrigerate for up to 2 weeks. **MAKES 2 CUPS (500ML)**

RANCH DRESSING
Whisk to combine ½ cup (150g) reduced-fat whole-egg mayonnaise, ½ cup (125ml) buttermilk, 1 tablespoon Dijon mustard, 2 tablespoons finely grated parmesan, ¼ cup snipped chives, 1 tablespoon lemon juice, salt and pepper. Refrigerate for up to 10 days. **MAKES 1½ CUPS (375ML)**

CORIANDER DRESSING
Place 1 cup coriander (cilantro) leaves, 2 sliced spring onions (scallions), 1 tablespoon finely grated ginger and ¼ cup (60ml) each mirin* and rice wine vinegar* in a food processor or blender and process until finely chopped. Refrigerate for up to 5 days. **MAKES 1½ CUPS (375ML)**

MISO DRESSING
Mix to combine 2 tablespoons each white miso paste* and mirin*, 1 tablespoon rice wine vinegar* and 1 teaspoon sesame oil. Refrigerate for up to 10 days.
MAKES 100ML

GREEN TAHINI DRESSING
Place ⅔ cup (160ml) tahini paste*, ½ cup (125ml) water, ⅓ cup (80ml) lemon juice, 1 tablespoon white wine vinegar, 2 teaspoons honey, 1½ cups coriander (cilantro) leaves, 1 cup flat-leaf parsley leaves, 1 clove crushed garlic, salt and pepper in a food processor and process until smooth. Refrigerate for up to 2 weeks. MAKES 2 CUPS (500ML)

LEMON BUTTERMILK DRESSING
Whisk to combine ¾ cup (180ml) buttermilk, 2 tablespoons lemon juice, 1 teaspoon finely grated lemon rind, ¼ cup finely chopped flat-leaf parsley leaves, salt and pepper. Refrigerate for up to 10 days.
MAKES 1 CUP (250ML)

GINGER *and* CHILLI DIPPING SAUCE

SOY *and* SESAME DIPPING SAUCE

GINGER *and* CHILLI DIPPING SAUCE

2 tablespoons shredded ginger
1 large red chilli, seeds removed and thinly sliced
⅓ cup (70g) caster (superfine) sugar
¼ cup (60ml) water
2 tablespoons lime juice
1 tablespoon fish sauce*

Place the ginger, chilli, sugar, water, lime juice and fish sauce in a saucepan over medium heat. Simmer for 3–5 minutes or until slightly thickened. Cool before serving. MAKES 1 CUP (250ML)
+ *Serve with rice paper rolls, as a dipping sauce for dumplings, tossed through Asian salads or drizzled over steamed vegetables.*

SOY *and* SESAME DIPPING SAUCE

¼ cup (60ml) reduced-salt soy sauce
2 tablespoons Chinese rice wine* (Shaoxing) or sherry
1 teaspoon sesame oil
1 tablespoon caster (superfine) sugar
1 teaspoon grated ginger
¼ teaspoon Chinese five-spice powder*
1 teaspoon sesame seeds, toasted

Place the soy, wine, sesame oil, sugar, ginger, five-spice and sesame seeds in a saucepan over medium heat. Simmer for 3–5 minutes or until slightly thickened. Cool before serving. MAKES ⅓ CUP (80ML)
+ *Serve with rice paper rolls, as a dipping sauce for dumplings, tossed through Asian salads or drizzled over steamed vegetables.*

RICOTTA *with* LEMON *and* MINT + CHILLI *and* PEPPER

lemon and mint
1½ cups (300g) reduced-fat ricotta
1 tablespoon finely grated lemon rind
1 tablespoon chopped mint leaves
chilli and pepper
1½ cups (300g) reduced-fat ricotta
¼ teaspoon dried chilli flakes
¼ teaspoon cracked black pepper

To make the lemon and mint ricotta, place the ricotta, lemon rind and mint in a bowl and mix well to combine.

To make the chilli and pepper ricotta, place the ricotta, chilli and pepper in a bowl and mix well to combine. Store in an airtight container in the refrigerator for up to 1 week. MAKES 1½ CUPS (300G)
+ *Serve this ricotta spread on toast or bruschetta as a snack, tossed through pasta or as a dip with crunchy vegetables. These make a great alternative to butter in a sandwich, too.*

Ricotta is such an all-round star in the kitchen and is EXCELLENT in both sweet and SAVOURY dishes. I've used it in many desserts but it's also great for snacks. It makes a great blank CANVAS for many flavours – try it with lemon rind, chilli or fresh herbs.

RICOTTA *with* LEMON *and* MINT + CHILLI *and* PEPPER

GLOSSARY *and* INDEX

Most of the INGREDIENTS in this book are sourced from supermarkets,
but if you're unsure of a particular ingredient, have a look in the GLOSSARY.
Ingredients marked with an asterisk are listed, as well as basic information on some
staple ingredients. There's also a useful list of global MEASURES, temperatures
and common CONVERSIONS. To make recipes easier to find in the book,
they are listed alphabetically in the INDEX and also by ingredient and dish.

agave syrup (nectar)
From the genus of succulent plants found in Mexico and South America, agave pulp is commonly used to make tequila or mezcal, while the syrup is used as a sweetener. Similar to honey, though not as runny, agave syrup can be used in baking and desserts instead of sugar.

almond meal
Also known as ground almonds, almond meal is available from most supermarkets. Make your own by processing whole skinned almonds to a fine meal in a food processor or blender (125g almonds will give 1 cup almond meal). To remove the skins from almonds, soak in boiling water, then, using your fingers, slip the skins off.

baba ghanoush
A creamy Middle Eastern dip of pureéd roasted eggplant, garlic, lemon juice, cumin and tahini (sesame seed paste) commonly served on a mezze platter with flatbread, for dipping. It has a distinct smoky flavour.

barley
pearl
Is a polished, milled form of barley grain, commonly added to soups and stews.

rolled
This is steamed and flattened barley used to make porridge or added to baked goods.

butter
Unless stated otherwise in a recipe, butter should be at room temperature for cooking. It should not be half-melted or too soft to handle, but should still have some 'give' when pressed.

butter beans
Large, plump white beans also known as lima beans. They go well in soups, stews and salads. Available from delicatessens and supermarkets either canned or in dried form. Dried beans need to be soaked in water before cooking.

capers
The small green flower buds of the caper bush. Available packed either in brine or salt. Use salt-packed capers when possible, as the texture is firmer and the flavour superior. Before use, rinse thoroughly, drain and pat dry.

caramelised onion relish
Sliced onion cooked slowly to release all its sugars and made even more intense in flavour by the addition of brown sugar and balsamic vinegar. It is sold in most supermarkets as a condiment.

cheese
goat's cheese & curd
Goat's milk has a tart flavour, so cheese made from it, sometimes labelled 'chèvre', has a sharp, slightly acidic taste. Immature goat's cheese is milder and creamier than mature cheese and is sometimes found labelled 'goat's curd'. Goat's cheese is also available in hard and soft varieties.

gruyére
Firm cow's milk cheese with a smooth ivory interior and a natural brushed rind. Popular in Switzerland as a table cheese and cooked into fondues, gratins and quiches. It makes a fabulous melting cheese, especially in a sandwich.

haloumi
Firm white Cypriot cheese made from sheep's milk. It has a stringy texture and is usually sold in brine. Available from delicatessens and some supermarkets. Holds its shape during grilling and frying.

labna
Middle Eastern cheese made from strained yoghurt based on cow's milk. See *yoghurt cheese* recipe, page 176.

mozzarella
Italian in origin, mozzarella is the mild cheese of pizza, lasagne and tomato salads. It's made by cutting and spinning (or stringing) the curd to achieve a smooth, elastic consistency. The most prized variety is made from buffalo's milk.

parmesan
Italy's favourite hard, granular cheese is made from cow's milk. Parmigiano reggiano is the 'Rolls-Royce' variety, made under strict guidelines in the Emilia-Romagna region and aged for an average of two years. Grana padano mainly comes from Lombardy and is aged for 15 months.

ricotta
A creamy, finely grained white cheese. Ricotta means 'recooked' in Italian, a reference to the way the cheese is produced by heating the whey left over from making other cheese varieties. It's fresh and creamy and low in fat and there is also a reduced-fat version, which is lighter again.

chermoula
This is a spicy Moroccan marinade or seasoning made from many spices including chilli, cumin and coriander as well as preserved lemon rind, garlic and herbs. It's often used to coat fish or chicken or is used to make a sauce.

chickpeas (garbanzos)
A legume native to western Asia and across the Mediterranean, the chickpea is used in soups, stews and is the base ingredient in the Middle Eastern dip, hummus. Dried chickpeas must be soaked before cooking, but you can also buy them canned.

chilli jam
Thai condiment made from ginger, chilli, garlic and shrimp paste used in soups and stir-fries. It goes well with roasted meats, egg dishes and cheese and is often served in a dollop as a garnish.

chillies
There are over 200 different types of chilli in the world. By general rule of thumb, long red or green chillies are milder, fruitier and sweeter, while small chillies are much hotter. Remove the membranes and seeds for a milder result in a dish.

chinese black beans
Also known as fermented black beans, these small black soy beans are fermented in salt and spices and are used as a robust seasoning in stir-fries and braised dishes. The beans should be rinsed before using.

chinese cooking wine (shaoxing)

Similar to dry sherry, Shaoxing or Chinese cooking wine is a blend of glutinous rice, millet, a special yeast and the local spring waters of Shaoxing, where it is made, in northern China. It is sold in the Asian aisle of your supermarket and in Asian grocery stores.

chinese five-spice powder

A blend of cinnamon, Sichuan pepper, star anise, clove and fennel seeds. Available at Asian food stores and supermarkets.

chipotle chilli

This is a dried, smoked version of a jalapeño pepper, with a distinct medium–hot flavour. They must be soaked in water before using.

coconut

cream

The cream that rises to the top after the first pressing of coconut milk. Coconut cream is a rich, sweet liquid that is both higher in energy and fat than regular coconut milk. A common ingredient in curries and Asian sweets.

milk

A milky, sweet liquid made by soaking grated fresh coconut flesh or desiccated coconut in warm water and squeezing through muslin or cheesecloth to extract the liquid. Available in cans or freeze-dried from supermarkets, coconut milk should not be confused with coconut juice, which is a clear liquid found inside young coconuts and often served as a refreshing drink in Asia.

coriander (cilantro)

This pungent green herb is common in Asian and Mexican cooking. The finely chopped roots are sometimes incorporated in curry pastes. The dried seeds are an Indian staple, sold ground or whole, and one of the base ingredients in curry. The dried form can not be substituted for fresh.

couscous

The name given to both the national dish of Algeria, Tunisia and Morocco and the tiny grains of flour-coated semolina that make it.

dijon mustard

Also known as French mustard, this is a pale, creamy and mildly flavoured mustard. It's commonly used in a vinaigrette.

eggs

The standard egg size used in this book is 60g. It is important to use the right size eggs for a recipe, as this will affect the outcome of baked goods. The correct volume is especially important when using eggwhites to make meringues. You should use eggs at room temperature for baking.

farro

A dried grain similar to pearl barley. When cooked it becomes chewy and nutty. You can find it at Italian grocery stores and health food stores.

fennel

With a mild aniseed flavour and crisp texture, fennel bulb is ideal for salads or roasting with meat or fish. The roasted version sweetens during cooking and goes very well with roasted pork.

fish sauce

An amber-coloured liquid drained from salted, fermented fish and used to add flavour to Thai and Vietnamese dishes such as curries and in dressings for salads. There are different grades available.

flatbread

There are many types of Middle Eastern flatbreads available, from small or large round pide or Lebanese bread, which can act as 'pockets' for fillings, to long loaves of Afghan and Turkish bread.

flaxseed

Also known as linseeds, flaxseeds are high in fibre, anti-oxidants and omega 3 fatty acids and are available in seed or oil form from health food shops as well as the health food aisle in some supermarkets.

flour

Made from ground cereal grains, flour is the primary ingredient in breads, cakes and many other baked goods including biscuits, pastries, pizzas and pie cases.

cornflour (cornstarch)

When made from ground corn or maize, cornflour is a gluten-free flour. It is often blended with water or stock to use as a thickening agent. Not to be confused with cornflour in the United States, which is finely ground corn meal.

plain (all-purpose)

Ground from the endosperm of wheat, plain white flour contains no raising agent.

rice

A fine flour made from ground white rice. Used as a thickening agent, in baking and to coat foods when cooking Asian dishes, particularly those needing a crispy finish.

self-raising (self-rising)

Ground from the endosperm of wheat, self-raising flour contains raising agents including sodium carbonates and calcium phosphates. To make it using plain flour, add 1½ teaspoons of baking powder for every 150g of flour.

whole-wheat

Derived by grinding or mashing the whole grain of wheat, whole-wheat flour refers to the fact that all of the grain (bran, germ and endosperm) is used and nothing is lost in the process of making the flour. It gives baked goods a unique body and flavour. Available from health food stores.

gai larn

Also known as Chinese broccoli or Chinese kale, gai larn is a leafy vegetable with dark green leaves, small flowers and stout stems.

gelatine

Available as a powder or in leaf form, gelatine is a setting agent made from collagen. It must be dissolved in cold water before being added to the recipe.

gowgee wrappers

Chinese in origin, these square thin sheets of dough are available fresh or frozen. They can be steamed or fried. Fill them with meat, vegetables and herbs to make dumplings for soup. See also *wonton wrappers*.

harissa

A North African condiment, harissa is a hot red paste made from chilli, garlic and spices including coriander, caraway and cumin. It may also contain tomato. Available in jars and tubes from supermarkets and specialty food stores, harissa enlivens tagines and couscous dishes and can be added to dressings, sauces and marinades.

horseradish

A pungent root vegetable that releases mustard oil when cut or grated. Commonly sold as grated horseradish or horseradish cream. A superb partner for pork and roast beef. Available fresh from greengrocers or in jars from the supermarket.

kaffir lime leaves

Fragrant leaves with a distinctive double-leaf structure, used crushed or shredded in Thai dishes. Available fresh or dried from Asian food stores.

kecap manis

An Indonesian soy sauce sweetened with palm sugar, it is thicker and sweeter than normal soy sauce and is commonly used in stir-fries and noodle dishes.

lemongrass

A tall lemon-scented grass used in Asian cooking, particularly in Thai dishes. Peel away the outer leaves and chop the tender white root-end finely, or add in large pieces during cooking and remove before serving. If adding in large pieces, bruise them with the back of a large knife.

LSA

A combination of linseed (flaxseed), sunflower seed and almond, which is made into a ground meal. It's an excellent source of protein and fibre and can be added to cereal, yoghurt and baked goods.

maple syrup

A sweetener made from the sap of the maple tree. Be sure to use pure maple syrup rather than imitation or pancake syrup, which is made from corn syrup flavoured with maple and does not have the same intensity of flavour.

mirin

A pale yellow Japanese cooking wine made from glutinous rice and alcohol. Sweet mirin is flavoured with corn syrup.

miso paste

A traditional Japanese ingredient produced by fermenting rice, barley or soy beans, with salt and fungus to a thick paste. It is used for sauces and spreads, pickling vegetables or meats, and mixing with dashi soup stock to serve as miso soup. Red miso paste is robust while white miso paste is more delicate in flavour. Available from supermarkets and Asian food stores.

noodles

Keep a supply of dried noodles in the pantry for last-minute meals. Fresh noodles will keep in the fridge for a week. Available from supermarkets and Asian food stores.

cellophane (bean thread)

Also called mung bean vermicelli or glass noodles, these noodles are very thin and almost transparent. Soak them in boiling water and drain well to prepare for use.

dried rice

Fine, dried noodles common in southeast Asian cooking. Depending on their thickness, rice noodles need only be boiled briefly, or soaked in hot water until soft.

rice vermicelli

Very thin dried rice noodles sometimes called rice sticks. They are usually used in soups such as laksa and in salads.

soba

Japanese noodles made from buckwheat and wheat flour, soba are greyish brown in colour and served both hot and cold.

udon

This thick Japanese wheat noodle is commonly used in soups.

nori

Used mainly for sushi rolls or crushed and sprinkled over salads, nori is an edible seaweed that's toasted and sold in sheets from Asian grocery stores.

oat bran

The outer casing of an oat, oat bran is high in fibre and can be used in baked goods or breakfast cereal or porridge. It can be used in muffins, cookies, savoury pancakes and more as a healthy alternative to flour.

olives

black

Black olives are more mature and less salty than the green variety. Choose firm olives with good colour and a fruity taste.

green

Green olives are picked when unripe, which makes them denser in texture than black olives. The Sicilian variety of green olives are plump and fruity.

oil

Olive oil is graded according to its flavour, aroma and acidity. Extra virgin is the highest quality oil; it contains no more than 1 per cent acid. Virgin is the next best; it contains 1.5 per cent or less acid and may have a slightly fruitier taste than extra virgin. Bottles labelled 'olive oil' contain a combination of refined and unrefined virgin olive oil. Light olive oil is the least pure in quality and intensity of flavour.

tapenade

Paste made by blending olives, capers, garlic and anchovies with oil. Served as a dip with crackers, or spread on bruschetta and pizzas, it makes a good marinade and partner for cold meat or cheeses.

pancetta

A cured Italian meat that is like prosciutto but less salty and with a softer texture. It's sold as round pancetta that has been rolled and is then sliced. It's perfect grilled until crispy and added to salad, pasta or risotto. Also sold as an unrolled piece called flat pancetta, which you can chop and use like other cured pork products such as speck.

pastry
filo (phyllo)

Extremely thin sheets of pastry popular in Greek, Turkish and Middle Eastern baking, particularly for sweets.

shortcrust

A savoury or sweet pastry that is available ready-made in blocks and frozen sheets. Keep a supply or make your own pastry.

1½ cups (225g) plain (all-purpose) flour
125g butter, chilled and cut into cubes
3 egg yolks
1 tablespoon iced water
Place the flour and butter in the bowl of a food processor and process in short bursts until mixture resembles fine breadcrumbs. While the motor is running, add the egg yolks and water. Process until the dough just comes together. Turn dough out onto a lightly floured surface and gently bring together to form a ball. Using your hands, flatten dough into a disc. Cover in plastic wrap and refrigerate. When ready to use, roll out on a lightly floured surface to 3mm thick. To make sweet shortcrust pastry, add ½ cup (80g) icing (confectioner's) sugar.

pickled ginger

Also known as gari, this Japanese condiment is made from young ginger that's been pickled in sugar and vinegar. It's commonly served with sushi.

pistachio

A delicately flavoured green nut inside a hard outer shell, pistachios are available salted or unsalted. They're used in Middle Eastern cuisine as well as in salads and sweets, such as baklava.

preserved lemon

Preserved lemons are lemons rubbed with salt, packed in jars, covered with lemon juice and left for about four weeks. They're often flavoured with cloves, cinnamon or chilli. Discard the flesh, rinse and chop the rind for use in cooking. They are popular in Moroccan cuisine, where they are added to tagines, and they also make a zesty salad dressing. Available from delicatessens and speciality food stores.

prosciutto

Italian ham that's been salted and dried for up to two years. The paper-thin slices are eaten raw or used to lend their distinctive flavour to braises and other cooked dishes. Often used to wrap figs or melon as part of an antipasto platter.

polenta

Used extensively in northern Italy, this corn meal is cooked in simmering water until it has a porridge-like consistency. In this form it is enriched with butter and cheese to serve with meat dishes. Otherwise it is left to cool, cut into squares and grilled, fried or baked.

puy lentils

Grown in the Le Puy region of France, this small slate-green lentil holds its shape well during cooking and has a unique peppery and nutty flavour. It's great in warm or cold salads and soups.

quinoa

Although quinoa looks like a grain, it's actually a seed originating from South America. Packed with protein, it has a chewy texture and nutty flavour and is fluffy when cooked. The most common variety is white, which is mild in taste, while the red variety has a stronger flavour and crunch. You can use it as you would couscous or rice.

flakes

This is quinoa simply steam rolled into flakes. They can be used in breakfast cereal, pancakes or baked goods. Available from health food stores.

sesame seeds

These small seeds have a strong nutty flavour. White sesame seeds are the most common variety, but black, or unhulled, seeds are popular for coatings in Asian cooking as well as some Asian desserts. Sesame oil is made by extracting the oil from roasted seeds.

silver beet

Also known as Swiss chard, this spinach has deep green leaves and also comes in a coloured variety with a pretty rhubarb hue.

smoked paprika

Unlike Hungarian paprika, the Spanish style known as pimentón is deep and smoky in flavour. It is made from smoked, ground pimiento peppers and comes in varying intensities from sweet and mild (dulce), bittersweet medium hot (agridulce) and hot (picante).

speck

Speck is a slab of German-style smoked and cured ham and is available from delicatessens. If unavailable, you can use bacon or flat pancetta instead.

spelt

Spelt is an ancient grain that is lower in gluten than wheat. It also has fewer calories and higher protein than regular flour. Like rolled oats, spelt oats or flakes are commonly used to make porridge.

star anise

A small brown seed-cluster that is shaped like a star. It has a strong aniseed flavour and can be used whole or ground in sweet and savoury dishes. It works well in master stocks or braises.

sugar

Extracted as crystals from the juice of the sugar cane plant or beet, sugar is a sweetener, flavour enhancer, bulking agent and preservative.

brown

Processed with molasses, it comes in differing shades of brown, according to the quantity of molasses added, which varies between countries. This also affects the taste of the sugar, and therefore the end product.

caster (superfine)

Gives baked products a light texture and crumb, which is important for many cakes and light desserts such as meringues. It dissolves easily.

icing (confectioner's)

Regular granulated sugar ground to a very fine powder. It often clumps together and needs to be sieved before using. Use pure icing sugar not icing sugar mixture, which contains cornflour (cornstarch) and needs more liquid.

white

Regular granulated sugar is used in baking when a light texture is not crucial. The crystals are large, so you need to beat, add liquids or heat this sugar to dissolve it.

sumac

Dried berries of a flowering plant are ground to produce an acidic reddish-purple powder popular in the Middle East.

sweet potato (kumara)

Long, tuberous root available in white- and orange-fleshed varieties. The orange sweet potato, also known as kumara, is sweeter and moister than the white. Both varieties can be roasted, boiled or mashed.

tahini paste

A thick paste made from ground sesame seeds. Used in Middle Eastern cooking, it is available in jars and cans from supermarkets and health food shops. It is used to make the popular dip hummus.

tarragon

Called the king of herbs by the French and used in many of their classic sauces such as Bernaise and tartare. It has a slight aniseed flavour and works well with scrambled eggs.

thai curry paste

Buy good-quality pastes in jars from Asian food stores or the supermarket. When trying a new brand, it is a good idea to add a little at a time to test the heat as the chilli intensity can vary significantly from brand to brand.

tins

Aluminium (aluminum) tins are fine but stainless steel will last longer and won't warp or buckle. Always measure widths across the base of the tin.

muffin

The standard sizes are a 12-hole tin: each hole with ½ cup (125ml) capacity; or a 6-hole tin, each hole with 1 cup (250ml) capacity. Mini-muffin tins have a capacity of 1½ tablespoons. Non-stick tins make for easy removal, or line with paper cases.

round

The standard sizes for round tins are 18cm, 20cm, 22cm and 24cm. The 20cm and 24cm tins are must-haves.

springform

The standard sizes for springform tins are 18cm, 20cm, 22cm and 24cm. The 20cm and 24cm round tins are the must-have members of the range.

square

The standard sizes for square tins are 18cm, 20cm, 22cm and 24cm. If you have a recipe for a cake cooked in a round tin and you want to use a square tin, the general rule is to subtract 2cm from the size of the tin. For example, you would need a 20cm square tin for a recipe calling for a 22cm round cake tin.

tofu

Literally translated as 'bean curd', tofu is made by coagulating the milk of soy beans and pressing the curd into blocks. Tofu comes in several grades according to the amount of moisture that has been removed. Silken tofu is the softest, with a custard-like texture. Soft tofu is slightly firmer, while dried or firm tofu has the texture of, and cuts like, a semi-hard cheese such as haloumi. Usually sold in the refrigerated section of supermarkets.

tomato

bottled tomato pasta sauce

Sometimes labelled 'passata' or 'sugo'. Italian for 'passed', passata is made by removing the skins and seeds from ripe tomatoes and passing the flesh through a sieve to make a thick, rich, pulpy tomato purée. Sugo is made from crushed tomatoes, so it has a little more texture than passata. Both are available in bottles from supermarkets.

heirloom

A non-hybrid cultivar of tomato usually not grown on a commerical scale, heirlooms are large with a bumpy appearance and good, strong flavour. You can find heirloom tomatoes in rich reds, green and yellow.

paste

This triple-concentrated tomato purée is used as a flavour booster and thickener in soups, sauces and stews. There are also salt-reduced versions available.

purée

Canned puréed tomatoes (not tomato paste). Substitute with fresh or canned peeled and puréed tomatoes.

sun-dried

Tomato pieces that have been dried with salt, which dehydrates the fruit and concentrates the flavour. Available plain or packed in oil. These are great chopped into salads or pastas for an extra tomato flavour boost. You can also find semi-dried varieties which are plumper and more juicy.

tzatziki

Greek dip made from thick plain yoghurt, garlic and chopped or grated cucumber, sometimes with dill added. Available in supermarkets, it can also be used as a sauce for grilled meat and seafood or served as an accompaniment to savoury pastries. To make your own:

1 Lebanese cucumber, grated
1 cup (280g) thick plain yoghurt
¼ cup chopped mint leaves
1 tablespoon chopped dill
sea salt and cracked black pepper
Squeeze excess liquid from the cucumber. Place in a bowl with the yoghurt, mint, dill, salt and pepper and mix to combine. Serve as a thick dressing or sauce. Refrigerate for up to 10 days. Makes 1½ cups (375g).

vanilla beans

These fragrant cured pods from the vanilla orchid are used whole, often split with the tiny seeds inside scraped into the mixture, to infuse flavour into custard and cream-based recipes. They offer a rich and rounded vanilla flavour. If unavailable, substitute 1 vanilla bean with 1 teaspoon pure vanilla extract (a dark, thick liquid – not essence) or store-bought vanilla bean paste.

vanilla extract

For a pure vanilla taste, use a good-quality vanilla extract, not an essence or imitation flavour, or use a fresh vanilla bean or vanilla bean paste.

vinegar

balsamic

Originally from Modena in Italy, there are many varieties on the market ranging in quality and flavour. Aged balsamics are generally preferable. Also available in a milder white version, which is used in dishes where the colour is important.

balsamic glaze

A thick and syrupy reduction of balsamic vinegar and sugar available from supermarkets.

cider

Usually made from cider or apple must, cider vinegar has a golden amber hue and a sour appley flavour. Use it in dressings, marinades and chutneys.

malt

Made by malting barley, malt vinegar is light brown in colour and is a traditional flavouring for fish and chips or crisps in the UK. It's great used as a condiment or for pickling vegetables.

rice wine

Made from fermenting rice or rice wine, rice vinegar is milder and sweeter than vinegars made by oxidising distilled alcohol or wine made from grapes. Rice wine vinegar is available in white (colourless to pale yellow), black and red varieties from Asian food stores and some supermarkets.

white balsamic

Traditional balsamic vinegar is made with red wine while this variety is made with white wine. It is milder in flavour and is not as sweet as its dark cousin. It is used in sauces and dressings when you don't want a dark balsamic to colour your dish.

white wine

This common table vinegar is made from distilled white wine.

wasabi

A very hot Japanese paste similar to horseradish, wasabi is used in making sushi and as a condiment. It's available from Asian food stores and supermarkets.

wheat bran

The hard outer layer of the wheat grain, wheat bran is usually found in cereals and can be baked into muffins. Available from health food stores.

wheat germ

Wheat germ is part of the wheat kernel that is very high in protein. It can be added to muffins, pancakes, cereals, yoghurt, smoothies, cookies and baked goods.

white anchovies

These Spanish anchovies called 'boquerones' are filleted and marinated in white vinegar and olive oil, giving them a sweet, mild taste. They are popular as a tapas dish on their own and are great in robust salads.

white (cannellini) beans

These small, kidney-shaped beans are available from supermarkets either canned or in dried form. Dried beans need to be soaked overnight in water before cooking.

wonton wrappers

Chinese in origin, these square or round thin sheets of dough are available fresh or frozen. They can be steamed or fried. Fill them with meat and vegetables to make dumplings for soup or use as a crunchy base for nibbles, or deep-fry or bake and sprinkle with sugar for dessert.

xo sauce

Consumed mainly as a condiment, XO sauce is a seafood sauce invented in Hong Kong and is made of roughly chopped dried scallops, dried fish and shrimp, which is cooked with Yunnan ham, chilli, onion and garlic. It is considered a delicacy in China.

za'atar

Middle Eastern spice mix containing dried herbs, sesame seeds and sumac. Often used as a crust for grilled and baked meats.

GLOBAL MEASURES

measures vary from Europe
to the US and even from
Australia to NZ.

METRIC *and* IMPERIAL

Measuring cups and spoons may vary
slightly from one country to another,
but the difference is generally not
sufficient to affect a recipe. All cup and
spoon measures are level. An Australian
measuring cup holds 250ml (8 fl oz).

One Australian metric teaspoon
holds 5ml, one Australian tablespoon
holds 20ml (4 teaspoons). However, in
North America, New Zealand and the UK
they use 15ml (3-teaspoon) tablespoons.

When measuring liquid ingredients
remember that 1 American pint contains
500ml (16 fl oz), but 1 Imperial pint
contains 600ml (20 fl oz).

When measuring dry ingredients,
add the ingredient loosely to the cup
and level with a knife. Don't tap or
shake to compact the ingredient unless
the recipe requests 'firmly packed'.

LIQUIDS *and* SOLIDS

measuring cups and spoons
and a set of scales are great
assets in the kitchen.

LIQUIDS

cup	metric	imperial
⅛ cup	30ml	1 fl oz
¼ cup	60ml	2 fl oz
⅓ cup	80ml	2½ fl oz
½ cup	125ml	4 fl oz
⅔ cup	160ml	5 fl oz
¾ cup	180ml	6 fl oz
1 cup	250ml	8 fl oz
2 cups	500ml	16 fl oz
2¼ cups	560ml	20 fl oz
4 cups	1 litre	32 fl oz

SOLIDS

metric	imperial
20g	½ oz
60g	2 oz
125g	4 oz
180g	6 oz
250g	8 oz
500g	16 oz (1 lb)
1kg	32 oz (2 lb)

MADE TO MEASURE

equivalents for metric and
imperial measures and
ingredient names.

MILLIMETRES TO INCHES

metric	imperial
3mm	⅛ inch
6mm	¼ inch
1cm	½ inch
2.5cm	1 inch
5cm	2 inches
18cm	7 inches
20cm	8 inches
23cm	9 inches
25cm	10 inches
30cm	12 inches

INGREDIENT EQUIVALENTS

bicarbonate soda	baking soda
capsicum	bell pepper
caster sugar	superfine sugar
celeriac	celery root
chickpeas	garbanzos
coriander	cilantro
cos lettuce	romaine lettuce
cornflour	cornstarch
eggplant	aubergine
green onion	scallion
plain flour	all-purpose flour
rocket	arugula
self-raising flour	self-rising flour
snow pea	mange tout
zucchini	courgette

OVEN TEMPERATURE

setting the oven to the right
temperature can be critical
when making baked goods.

CELSIUS TO FAHRENHEIT

celsius	fahrenheit
100°C	200°F
120°C	250°F
140°C	275°F
150°C	300°F
160°C	325°F
180°C	350°F
190°C	375°F
200°C	400°F
220°C	425°F

ELECTRIC TO GAS

celsius	gas
110°C	¼
130°C	½
140°C	1
150°C	2
170°C	3
180°C	4
190°C	5
200°C	6
220°C	7
230°C	8
240°C	9
250°C	10

BUTTER *and* EGGS

let 'fresh is best' be your
mantra when it comes
to selecting dairy goods.

BUTTER

For baking we generally use unsalted
butter as it lends a sweeter flavour.
Either way, the impact is minimal. Salted
butter has a longer shelf life and is preferred
by some people. One American stick of
butter is 125g (4 oz). One Australian
block of butter is 250g (8 oz).

EGGS

Unless otherwise indicated we use large
(60g) chicken eggs. To preserve freshness,
store eggs in the refrigerator in the carton
they are sold in. Use only the freshest
eggs in recipes such as mayonnaise or
dressings that use raw or barely cooked
eggs. Be extra cautious if there is a
salmonella problem in your community,
particularly in food that is to be served to
children, the elderly or pregnant women.

THE BASICS

here are some simple weight
conversions for cups of
common ingredients.

COMMON INGREDIENTS

almond meal (ground almonds)
1 cup | 120g
brown sugar
1 cup | 175g
white sugar
1 cup | 220g
caster (superfine) sugar
1 cup | 220g
icing (confectioner's) sugar
1 cup | 160g
plain (all-purpose)
or self-raising
(self-rising) flour
1 cup | 150g
fresh breadcrumbs
1 cup | 70g
finely grated parmesan cheese
1 cup | 80g
uncooked rice
1 cup | 200g
cooked rice
1 cup | 165g
uncooked couscous
1 cup | 200g
cooked, shredded chicken, pork or beef
1 cup | 160g
olives
1 cup | 150g

A

B

C

F

G

H

I

K

L

THANK YOU

Compared to the continuous loop sprint of a bi-monthly magazine, a book is like a marathon. Each year the team who sign up to work on it prepare themselves for the distance. I can only write recipes when there is calm and quiet, so for me it's a long stretch of late nights once my boys are in bed and lots of bleary eyed early morning starts. But I'm not the only one, and that's why I'm expressing my sincere gratitude to the following people.

Thank you Chi, for my beautiful new design and for the hours spent meticulously correcting proofs. You're such a lovely, calm perfectionist, and an absolute joy to work with. Thanks to my great friend William, for your beautiful photography. The true craftsman, your work is always technically correct and absolutely lovely, resulting in pages of stunning images. Thanks Hannah, for the persistence to make the sometimes seemingly impossible recipe not only work, but simple to cook as well. Thanks for keeping many of my styling days in the studio on track.

Thank you to my copy editor, Mel, for the long weekends of careful subbing and clever writing, beating every single word into shape. To my magazine team, thanks for being the quirky, creative and inspiring force that you are. Thanks also to Elke for your endless energy and jumping in when needed, as well as Holly for sourcing the beautiful products for these pages. A big thank you must also go to the team at HarperCollins for their ongoing support.

I would be lost without the support of all of my amazing friends – you know who you are. To my sister Karen, thank goodness you are my back up. And lastly, thanks to my little boys, Angus and Tom, the loves of my life.

Thank you to the following suppliers for the loan of their wares: Design Mode International (Jia, Iitalla and Hoganas Keramik), Georg Jensen, Jarass (Eva Solo, Holmegaard), MUD Australia, Pure Linen, Ondene, Riedel.

BIOGRAPHY

At the age of eight, Donna Hay skipped into a kitchen, picked up a mixing bowl and never looked back. She later moved to the world of magazine test kitchens and publishing, where she established her trademark style of simple, smart and seasonal recipes all beautifully put together and photographed.

It is food for every cook, every food-lover, every day and every occasion. Her unique style turned her into an international food-publishing phenomenon as a best-selling author of 20 cookbooks, publisher of the bi-monthly *donna hay magazine*, weekly newspaper columnist, creator of homewares and a food range, and shop owner of the donna hay general store in Sydney, Australia.

Books by Donna Hay include *simple dinners, a cook's guide, fast, fresh, simple., Seasons, no time to cook, off the shelf, modern classics, instant entertaining, the simple essentials* collection and the *marie claire* cooking series.

donnahay.com

To find more Donna Hay cookbooks, recipes and homewares,
go to donnahay.com and find us on Facebook and Twitter.